AFRICA
AND THE
UNITED STATES

COUNCIL ON FOREIGN RELATIONS BOOKS

The Council on Foreign Relations, Inc. is a non-profit and non-partisan organization devoted to promoting improved understanding of international affairs through the free exchange of ideas. Its membership of about 1,700 persons throughout the United States is made up of individuals with special interest and experience in international affairs. The Council has no affiliation with, and receives no funding from, the United States government. The Council does not take any position on questions of foreign policy.

The Council publishes the quarterly journal, *Foreign Affairs*. In addition, from time to time, books and monographs written by members of the Council's research staff or visiting fellows, or commissioned by the Council, or (like this book) written by independent authors with critical review contributed by a Council study group, are published with the designation "Council on Foreign Relations Book" or "Council Paper on International Affairs." Any book or monograph bearing that designation is, in the judgment of the Committee on Studies of the Council's board of directors, a responsible treatment of a significant international topic worthy of presentation to the public. All statements of fact and expressions of opinion contained in Council books, monographs, and *Foreign Affairs* articles are, however, the sole responsibility of their authors.

AFRICA
AND THE
UNITED STATES:
Vital Interests

Edited by
JENNIFER SEYMOUR WHITAKER

A Council on Foreign Relations Book
Published by
New York University Press · New York · 1978

Copyright © 1978 by Council on Foreign Relations Inc.
Library of Congress Catalog Card Number: 77-92753

Library of Congress Cataloging in Publication
Main entry under title:

Africa and the United States.

"A Council on Foreign Relations book."
Includes bibliographical references and index.
    1. Africa—Relations (general) with the United
States—Addresses, essays, lectures.   2.   United States—
Relations (general) with Africa—Addresses, essays,
lectures.   I.   Whitaker, Jennifer Seymour, 1938-
DT38.A43   301.29'6073   77-92753
ISBN 0-8147-9181-6
ISBN 0-8147-9182-4 pbk.

Manufactured in the United States of America

Contents

Foreword

Senator Dick Clark

Once a continent with little international prominence, Africa now occupies a central focus among key foreign policy concerns. The turning point came, oddly enough, with a historic event in Europe. The Lisbon coup d'état in 1974 marked the end of Africa's last colonial empire and the beginning of a new strategic balance that has had worldwide implications.

It is obvious at this point that many of the assumptions that have guided our African policy in the past have proven to be patently false or seriously questionable. Prior to the Lisbon coup, we used to think that "white rule is here to stay" in southern Africa, but white rule not only has collapsed in Angola and Mozambique but is retreating in Rhodesia and Namibia. We used to think that Africa was an unlikely theater of great-power competition, but Soviet and American involvement is growing. We used to think that direct foreign intervention by nations outside sub-Saharan Africa was a remote possibility, but we have witnessed direct Cuban, Moroccan and French military intervention. We used to think that regional groups and alliances were relatively unimportant, but the five "front-line" states form a very significant political grouping in Africa today. Clearly, the United States needs to re-examine its policy toward Africa and the underlying assumptions that we held about its political and economic realities.

The Carter administration has also faced unpredicted foreign policy challenges that have had an impact far beyond the continent itself. Massive levels of Soviet and Cuban assistance to the Ethiopian regime in the conflict in the Ogaden revived the old and still unresolved debate on the meaning of U.S.-Soviet détente. Wars in the Western Sahara, Chad, and the Horn have presented dilemmas for U.S. policy, involving decisions on arms transfers, economic assistance, and diplomatic alliances. These three conflicts across the broad belt of Africa focus attention on increasing Arab interests in sub-Saharan Africa: an important dimension of the international politics of the continent highlighted by Moroccan intervention in Zaire, Algerian support of the Polisario Front, Libyan intervention in Chad, and by pressure from America's closest allies—Egypt, Iran and Saudi Arabia—for a stronger U.S. response in support of Somalia.

In southern Africa, fresh initiatives by the West to bring about negotiated settlements leading to majority rule in Rhodesia and Namibia have been frustrated by rival strategies developed by the white regimes that would install moderate governments in these two countries by the end of 1978—governments that would exclude the guerrilla movements. Domestic reaction to these developments has been divided. However, a growing segment of public opinion and congressional sentiment favors these settlements because, on the surface, they appear to offer peaceful pro-Western alternatives to military solutions that would invite greater Soviet and Cuban intervention and the spread of Marxism.

In reality, the internal solutions could do just the opposite. U.S. support for the internal settlements would almost certainly alienate many important African states, including the front-line countries and Nigeria, our second largest overseas supplier of oil and the continent's largest and most powerful country, with which we have been closely coordinating our Africa policy. Most seriously, however, the internal settlements could provoke a classic split into pro-Western and pro-Soviet camps that occurred previously in Angola. This would place the United States on the side of the Rhodesian whites and South Africa while the Soviet Union and Cuba backed the nationalists. The resulting situation would risk confrontation with Moscow, drive the liberation movements into greater dependency on the Communists, and accelerate the drift of events in the region into a general race war that could have serious repercussions in our own society. We are thus approaching what may be a crossroads in U.S. policy toward Africa that would determine the future of American influence in the continent for years.

Human rights, economic needs, ideological competition, foreign intervention, great-power rivalry, local conflict situations, and competing foreign policy interests are combining to provide the toughest tests yet of American credibility in Africa—tests not only of our obviously outdated assumptions, but also of our will, our principles, our perceptions, and our skill in responding to the challenges of a continent undergoing revolutionary transformations. These are tests that we cannot afford to fail.

The Council on Foreign Relations Discussion Group on U.S. Policy Toward Africa was an excellent forum for a reexamination of these issues. The meetings of the group took place in Washington, D.C., over a period of six months that began, appropriately, in the last month of the Nixon-Ford administration and continued on into the new Carter administration. A more fitting time could not have been chosen. The change in administrations brought with it a shift in U.S. foreign policy objectives that has had profound implications for Africa.

Seminar participants included a cross-section of representatives from Congress, the executive branch, academia, and the press—both the critics and the creators of policy. The papers presented and the discussions that took place during these meetings were the most thorough and penetrating survey of African policy issues that it has been my pleasure to experience. The essays in this book cover those issues most directly related to U.S. interests and policy. They should make a real contribution to the American approach to Africa in the years ahead. I consider it a privilege to have presided over these seminars, and I congratulate the Council on Foreign Relations for making these superb meetings possible.

March 30, 1978

CONTRIBUTORS

GORDON BERTOLIN was formerly a Peace Corps volunteer in Cameroon and recently completed graduate work in international economics at Columbia University. He is currently an International Development Intern for A.I.D. stationed in Upper Volta.

GUY F. ERB was a Senior Fellow at the Overseas Development Council until September 1977, when he joined the staff of the National Security Council. While at ODC he edited, with Valerina Kallab, *Beyond Dependency: The Developing World Speaks Out*, and wrote "Negotiations on Two Fronts: Manufactures and Commodities," among other publications.

I. WILLIAM ZARTMAN is Professor of Politics and former Department Head at New York University. He is the author of *International Politics in the New Africa*, among other books, and contributor of chapters on African political problems in *World Politics* (Rosenau, ed.), *African Diplomacy* (McKay, ed.), *Africa in the 1980s* (Morse, ed.), *Soldier and State in Africa* (Welch, ed.), and other works. He is currently completing a book on negotiation and starting a study of international crisis management in Africa.

GEOFFREY KEMP is Associate Professor of International Politics at The Fletcher School of Law and Diplomacy, Tufts University. He has served as a consultant to the Department of Defense and the Committee on Foreign Relations, U. S. Senate. He is currently at work on a book on U. S. maritime strategy.

ROBERT LEGVOLD is a Senior Research Fellow at the Council on Foreign Relations and Director of its U.S.-Soviet Relations Project. He is the author of *Soviet Policy in West Africa*.

ANDREW NAGORSKI is currently Asian Editor for *Newsweek International*, based in Hong Kong. Prior to that assignment, he served as a writer and editor based in New York and wrote frequently about southern Africa. In 1975, he received an Overseas Press Club citation for his September 15, 1974, cover story "Black Africa Moves South."

JENNIFER SEYMOUR WHITAKER is Associate Editor of *Foreign Affairs* and a Fellow specializing in Africa at the Council on Foreign Relations. She is the author of the Headline Series book, *Conflict in Southern Africa*.

[xi]

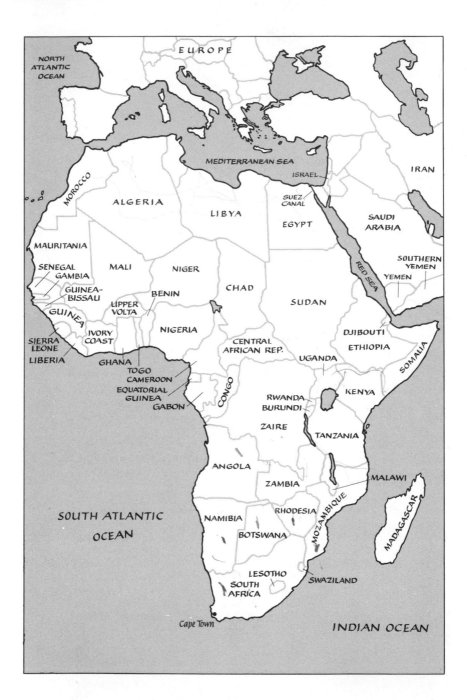

Introduction:
Africa and U.S. Interests

Jennifer Seymour Whitaker

From the mid-1960s until the mid-1970s, developments in the continent of Africa were largely ignored by higher-level foreign policy makers. The Congo crises of the early and mid-1960s, the consolidation of the one-party state as the most common form of nonmilitary government, and a succession of military coups across the continent combined to dash the sympathetic identification of Western liberals with the new African "democratic experiment." Black Africa came to be perceived as merely a collection of small, poor, authoritarian states, without much importance to international politics.

The United States during this time was increasingly preoccupied with the ultimately unsolvable problem of Vietnam but also, secondarily, with the Middle East. Vietnam left U.S. policy makers with little energy to expend on unrelated issues in other parts of the Third World, while the two Middle East wars drew the United States into a role as indirect military supplier for Portuguese counterinsurgency in Africa because Portugal's Azores bases had become the main refueling depot for U.S. planes flying to Israel.

By 1970, the desire of the war-weary United States for a stable status quo in Africa as well as its interest in reliable basing arrangements were evident in President Richard Nixon's and Secretary of State Henry A. Kissinger's analysis of the principal political issue in U.S.-African relations—the struggle between African nationalism and the white minority regimes in the southern part of the continent. Predicting that the superior power of the Portuguese, the Rhodesians and the South Africans would ensure their continued control of the area for the indefinite future, the Nixon-Kissinger administration opted for a "tilt" toward the white minority regimes. According to National Security Study Memorandum (NSSM) 39, the key to their policy was to be "communication" with South Africa. Beyond that, they paid little attention to events elsewhere on the continent. The U.S. indifference was made more comfortable by the apparently low level of Soviet interest in Africa during much of this period. (In fact, while the Soviet Union had by the late 1960s become quite cautious in its efforts to establish profitable relationships with potentially "revolutionary" regimes, it maintained a flow of aid to various of the southern African liberation movements throughout the decade.)

The 1974 coup in Portugal, however, and that nation's hasty withdrawal from its African colonies, destroyed the regional status quo, while simultaneously heightening Soviet interest. Belatedly, the United States tried to influence the power struggle in Angola by covertly backing a guerrilla movement opposing one aided by the Soviets. Congressional rejection of that stratagem and wholesale African endorsement of the Soviet- and Cuban-backed group after South Africa's intervention on behalf of the U.S.-backed faction led to a broad review of Africa policy within the administration. The upshot was a swift public turnabout, signalled in Secretary Kissinger's Lusaka speech of April 29, 1976, and in the African shuttle diplomacy which he maintained until his last days in office. At Lusaka, Mr. Kissinger for the first time committed the United States firmly to a policy of "majority rule" in Rhodesia and Namibia, and to the ending of "institutionalized separation of races" in South Africa itself. His diplomacy constituted a strenuous effort to maximize U.S. influence—and minimize that of the Soviets—over the transition to majority rule and the regimes which would take power as a result.

In the diplomatic arena, the Carter administration took the baton from Henry Kissinger, and has run further with it. It has also tried, with uncertain results, to de-emphasize the importance of superpower conflicts. In addition, Carter's concern for human rights has made racial injustice in southern Africa a primary focus. The unequivocal U.S. commitment to the end of apartheid was made clear to South Africa early on. Diplomacy, however, continues to be the main mode for achieving U.S. and Western goals. Thus, emphasis has been placed on "communication" with black African states in the various southern African conflicts, and cooperation with the pre-eminent regional power, Nigeria. In addition, we have paid heed to the voting weight and influence of the large African group in multilateral organizations. For all these reasons, a fair amount of attention is now being paid to African issues.

During the period of slackened U.S. interest in Africa, it was fashionable for policy analysts to conclude that the African continent was devoid of compelling interest for the United States. African experts lent credence to this view by generally absorbing themselves in the African scene and giving little thought to how it might affect U.S. interests or policy. Now that the United States finds itself involved anew in African issues, the need for informed analysis of U.S. foreign policy toward Africa is increasingly apparent. The purpose of this book is to determine the points of intersection between African issues and U.S. interests.

Africa is indeed vast, with heterogeneous political and ethnic traditions as well as varying economic potential. It is necessary, however, to view the continent as a whole in order to lay the groundwork for a sound U.S. policy. Although analysts often split Africa into "southern," or white-ruled, and "black" components we cannot define appropriate outlines for that policy without understanding that at this time in history, the entire continent is dominated by the last throes of decolonization.

The resolution of the conflict in southern Africa has been, and will continue to be, importantly affected by the policies and pressures of the countries of black Africa. Furthermore, the outcome in southern Africa will affect political developments in the rest of the continent for many years to come. Southern Africa weighs heavily on the United States in both our relations with the rest of the continent and our maneuvering vis-à-vis the Soviets. Conversely, our responses regarding southern Africa are shaped to a significant extent by interests in the rest of the continent, and our diplomatic opportunities in southern Africa flow from our relations with both black- and white-ruled Africa.

Physically, this region called Africa consists of 52 countries, most of them small and poor. They range in population from Nigeria with 80 million to the Seychelles Islands with 60,000 people; the median population is around 4 million. Excluding oil-rich Libya, per capita GNP ranges from $1,760 for Gabon and $1,200 for South Africa to $90 for Rwanda; the average is about $370.

These countries vary widely in endowments of natural resources, agricultural potential, and developed human resources. To finance development most African countries are still heavily dependent on agriculture and the export of agricultural goods. In black Africa, only South Africa can be said to be industrialized; Nigeria, with its sizable GNP ($28.8 billion), its increasingly educated population, and possible processing spinoffs from its oil industry, would appear to have the best prospects of any country in black Africa today for entering the ranks of industrialized nations.

Of Africa's approximately 420 million people, around 45 percent (that is, about 185 million) live in countries whose lingua franca is English; about 20 percent (or 82 million) live in countries where French is the main official language; about 15 million live in the former Portuguese colonies of Angola, Mozambique, and Guinea-Bissau; and a few Spanish areas comprise less than a million people. In addition, Arabic is the official language of about 23 percent, or 97 million people. Official African languages include Swahili (in Tanzania), Amharic (in Ethiopia), Malagasy, Somali, and Afrikaans. Most of the peoples of the continent commonly speak African languages, of which there are thought to be more than 2,000. Since achieving independence, the countries of black Africa have devoted large percentages of their resources to education, and today primary education is universal in almost half the countries of the continent.

While it is difficult to quantify accurately the religious affiliations, about 25 percent of Africans are said to be Christians, 40 percent Moslems, and the rest pagan or animist. In general, Islam has taken hold more firmly in the northern states of black Africa.

[5]

Almost half of sub-Saharan Africa is governed by military regimes; of the rest, most are one-party states. In both categories, degrees of state control and openness to outside investment vary widely. State ownership of major enterprises is extensive even in those states encouraging foreign investment, and a continuing trend toward public ownership is probable. Only a few, however, including Algeria, Mozambique, Angola, Guinea-Bissau, Congo, Somalia, Benin, and now perhaps Ethiopia, can yet be said to have looked to orthodox socialist models in organizing their economies and political systems. Tanzania has created its own form of African socialism, emphasizing equity and self-reliance.

U.S. interests intersect with African issues at three main points: in the quest for economic access to Africa's resources and investment opportunities; in North-South politics in the United Nations and other forums for multilateral negotiations; and in the internationalization of African conflicts. Gordon Bertolin's essay ("U.S. Economic Interests in Africa: Investment, Trade, and Raw Materials," Chapter 1) details the extent of U.S. dependency on African mineral resources and compares U.S. trade and investment figures for southern Africa with those in the rest of the continent. Both Bertolin and Geoffrey Kemp (in Chapter 4, "U.S. Strategic Interests and Military Options in Sub-Saharan Africa") discuss the threat to U.S. economic and strategic interests inherent in the southern African conflict. As both studies indicate, the most likely potential problem for the United States will be in possible sporadic disruptions of the market (both supply and pricing mechanisms), rather than in long-term cut-offs of supply. Regarding the scope for U.S. corporations in Africa, the propensity of many African governments to nationalize foreign enterprises has generated an uncertain investment climate. Multinationals have, however, found ways of adjusting to this situation, and in many cases still exert a good deal of control over their former enterprises in their new role as managers under contract to the African governments or the governments' parastatal corporations.[1] In South Africa, investment continues highly profitable though long-term stability must increasingly be called into question.

Guy Erb analyzes African economic interests in North-South politics in Chapter 2 ("Africa and the International Economy: A U.S. Response"). The main African preoccupation in international politics, after southern Africa, concerns the issue of a New International Economic Order (NIEO). Because 18 of the 29 states defined by the United Nations as least developed are African, there is, not surprisingly, a common emphasis among the nations of the African continent on the needs of the least developed. The bulk of African exports are concentrated in agricultural or mineral raw materials, and African countries have been particularly concerned about improving the terms of the commodities trade. Africans led the negotiations for the Lomé Agreement in 1975 between the European Community and its members' former African, Caribbean, and Pacific (ACP) dependencies, which created a system for compensating those countries with shortfalls in their revenues from commodities sales. Beyond this, some form of indexation (in which the prices of commodities exports would rise and fall with the prices of manufactured imports) and a common fund for commodities are considered to be general African goals in North-South negotiations. However, because a number of African countries do not export sufficient amounts of the given commodities to benefit from the fund, the African group has gone to the point of disrupting Fund negotiations to insist that "special measures" constituting general financing of development projects be included in the package. For most black African countries,

[7]

the issue of debt is relatively unimportant. Apart from Zaire, their debt and their ability to borrow are relatively small.

The diversity of interests within Africa between the poorest and the emerging middle-level economies (like Kenya, the Ivory Coast, the Cameroons, Gabon, Nigeria, Zambia, possibly Ghana, possibly Zaire, and eventually Zimbabwe) is wide and growing wider. Differences are partly masked, however, for several reasons. First, as was demonstrated in The Law of the Sea negotiations, for example, the poorest countries (which are mostly landlocked) have cast their lot, by and large, with the stronger African states (which are mostly coastal). Among other reasons, the poorest and weakest countries in Africa hardly have the manpower and expertise to devise and implement independent political strategies, even within the NIEO framework. Second, although the interests of the poorer nations often run counter to those of the coastal states, their great weakness has left them with only one seemingly viable strategy—dependence on the goodwill of their stronger neighbors. (That this strategy can pay off was seen in the African group's willingness to disrupt Common Fund negotiations which would benefit some of its members, in favor of aid mechanisms which would benefit all.)

At the United Nations the African caucus is organized around the regional Organization of African Unity (OAU). This group (which meets twice yearly) has given the caucus a good deal of cohesiveness on African political issues. Founded in 1963, the very name of the OAU expresses its creators' fervent goal. Few of its members have been willing to give up any of their sovereignty to the organization, but despite numerous differences, the OAU's commitment to (1) majority rule in southern Africa and (2) the maintenance of independent African sovereignties within the existing (colonial) boundaries has proven a strong bond until now. African peace-keeping was declared to be an African affair after the Congo operations of the United Nations. Before Angola, the prohibition against the involvement of outside powers in African conflicts had been broken chiefly by French interventions in Gabon, Mauritania, and Chad. Now, however, Soviet-Cuban operations in Angola and Ethiopia and direct Western military aid to Zaire appear to herald much more serious erosion of this principle.

African states constitute a third of the U.N. membership, and Africa's primary issue—the liberation of southern Africa—shares political priority with the Middle East. With regard to southern Africa, the African nations have placed the West, and particularly the United States, on the defensive over this pre-eminent human rights issue. From the mid-1960s until the mid-1970s, Western, and particularly U.S., foot-dragging on southern Africa was an important theme in what seemed a pattern of escalating North-South confrontation. Because of the implicit racial undertones in historical and contemporary relationships between the former colonial powers and the newly independent nations, the effect on North-South relations of an East-West confrontation over settlements in Zimbabwe and Namibia or of a race war in South Africa would be profound. Political abrasion inherent in the southern African situation will continue to seriously affect U.S.-African relations.

Until 1973 the African nations constituted a swing vote on Middle East questions in the United Nations, with pro-Arab votes preponderant, but in a sense balanced by pro-Israeli votes and abstentions combined.[2] Until then, African ties with the Arab world were balanced by largely friendly relationships with Israel—a consequence both of effective Israeli diplomacy and of African admiration for the ingenuity and hardihood of another small new nation. During 1972 and 1973, however,

[9]

African nations began breaking relations with Israel. Uganda, Chad, Congo-Brazzaville, Niger, Mali, Burundi, Togo, and Zaire severed relations before the Yom Kippur War; and all the rest, except Malawi, Swaziland and Lesotho (which maintain ties to the present) followed suit shortly thereafter.[3]

The virtually universal African rejection of Israel stemmed from a combination of several elements which came together in 1973, including: the mood of Third World unity and heightened anti-Western feelings stirred by the victory of the OPEC cartel; the implicit rewards promised by Afro-Arab solidarity at a time of extreme economic vulnerability; and sympathetic indentification with fellow liberationists, the Palestinians. For a time, in 1973 and 1974, the African group presented an almost solid pro-Arab phalanx (Malawi, Swaziland, Lesotho, and occasionally Botswana were exceptions) in General Assembly voting on Middle East resolutions. Over the next several years, however, OPEC aid to African countries was not as munificent as had been expected, and the aid was directed chiefly to a few Moslem states which belong to the Arab League, like Somalia and the Sudan and Mauritania. (There were additional small amounts to Mali, Senegal, and Guinea; Uganda also received substantial aid from Libya.) Since then the solid pro-Arab African phalanx has deteriorated to some extent, with the African group divided on the Zionist resolution in 1975 and, in response to heavy U.S. pressure, working behind the scenes to achieve a compromise on Israeli membership in UNESCO in 1976. Longer-term relationships between African and Arab states will in all likelihood see the growth of stronger links, particularly in the northern part of the continent, as well as continuing friction. The role of aid-donor is a relatively new one for the Arab OPEC states, but their neighboring African countries are a natural target for efforts to achieve wider influence.

A continuing irritant that produces pro-Arab or anti-Israeli attitudes in the African group is the increasingly close relationship between Israel and South Africa. A state visit by South African Prime Minister John Vorster to Jerusalem in 1976, followed by reports of nuclear cooperation and the sale of Israeli gunboats to South Africa, have increased African distrust of Israel.

For the decade and a half since Independence, Africa has been relatively free of internal conflicts. Now, however, this period of grace may be over, and a new era of intensified interstate conflict beginning. More than any other region of the world today, Africa is characterized by the fragility of national political institutions. The colonial glue which held things together for a time after Independence, both within states and at the boundaries between them, is now gradually dissolving. Its replacement by a new balancing of indigenous forces will be accompanied by a good deal of upheaval. William Zartman discusses the reasons for this change and some potential consequences in Chapter 3 ("Coming Political Problems in Black Africa").

Inevitably this jockeying for power will offer numerous opportunities for external aid, influence, and perhaps intervention. The strong African aversion to intervention by outside powers in African affairs—codified in the Charter of the OAU—will continue to act as a countervailing pressure. But this abstract principle held more power during the quest for national independence than in the present search for internal consolidation. In addition, it was easier to observe in peacetime than in times of war, and the present and potential conflicts on the continent are many. Those which have already drawn in

[11]

outside powers, or threatened to do so, include: the many-sided melee in the Horn of Africa, among Ethiopia, Somalia, Sudan, Kenya (and also Libya) and the Arabian peninsular states; the conflict over Western Sahara, pitting Morocco and Mauritania against Algeria and the Saharan Polisario liberation movement; the hostility between Zaire and its two neighbors, Angola and the Congo; the civil war in Chad; the collapse of East African cooperation; and finally, the conflicts in southern Africa.

The contemporary resurgence of ideology as a divisive factor among African states contributes to the international volatility of these disputes. Until now, most countries of Africa have declared their nonalignment in international politics, or neutrality regarding the conflicts of the great powers. Their economic and political ties have been strongest with the former European metropoles—Great Britain, France, Belgium, and Portugal. However, East-West alignments in Africa may be more clearly drawn in the future than in the recent past. Dependent on Soviet and Cuban aid for its very survival, Angola signed a treaty of friendship and cooperation with the Soviet Union in the spring of 1976. Like Angola, the other former Portuguese colonies, Mozambique and Guinea-Bissau, are Marxist in ideology, although they have relied somewhat less on the U.S.S.R. Mozambique also signed a treaty of friendship and cooperation in April 1977. After an abrupt leftward turn, Ethiopia broke with the United States in the spring of 1977 and called on the Soviet Union to help shore up its rather chaotic revolution. Subsequently, sizable contingents of Cuban troops were based in Ethiopia and deployed against the Somalis. On the other hand, particularly the Francophone countries like the Ivory Coast, Senegal, and Gabon are vigorously pro-Western in orientation. In addition, countries such as Kenya, Chad, Zaire, Sudan—and recently Somalia—are now voicing fears about the Soviet military role and have turned to the Western bloc for military aid.

I. William Zartman's and Robert Legvold's analyses of cold war and ideological divisions in Africa differ. Zartman does not see these trends as a particularly significant factor either in African political development or inter-African conflict. Legvold, however, looking at the continent from the Soviet perspective (in Chapter 5, "The Soviet Union's Strategic Stake in Africa") argues that increased Soviet political interest and military activity in Africa virtually necessitate a U.S.-Soviet military competition there.

The conflict on the Horn of Africa rivals that in southern Africa as a magnet for possible great-power interests and actions. Somalia's drive to incorporate all ethnic Somalis and the lands they inhabit into greater Somalia is the primary cause of the conflict. In addition, a variety of other ethnic and tribal disputes—principally within the boundaries of the other major antagonist, Ethiopia, but also involving Sudan, Kenya, and Libya—threaten to precipitate intra-state hostilities. Since Somalia became independent from Britain and Italy in 1960, the five-pointed star on its national flag has proclaimed an unabashed Somali irredentism. The five points stand for the five territories inhabited by ethnic Somalis, including the former British and Italian components of Somalia itself; newly independent Djibouti (formerly French Somaliland); Ethiopia's Ogaden region; and Kenya's Northern Frontier District (NFD) area. All these territories are claimed as part of greater Somalia.

Somalia's open irredentism has been unique in the post-Independence period, and has run counter to a strong OAU prohibition against tampering with the colonial borders, but the nation's efforts to annex portions of its neighbors' territory may encourage imitators. Although efforts to draw Djibouti (with its majority Somali population) into Somalia had been expected, the Somali army, with allied guerrillas, instead invaded Ethiopia's Ogaden in the summer of 1977. This move may have been hastened by the growing ties between Ethiopia's new revolutionary government, the Dergue, and Somalia's own patron, the Soviet Union. In the aftermath of the first successful Ogaden invasion Somalia itself executed a 180-degree turnabout in its external alliances, ejecting the Soviets from their naval bases at Berbera and expelling all Soviet and Cuban military advisors, while actively seeking arms and military aid from its conservative Arab allies and from the West. If Somalia had achieved its Ethiopian objectives either Djibouti or Kenya's NFD might have been the next target. (The still small Kenyan army—about 7,500 men versus Somalia's 23,000—would be hard put to defend this long border area.) The arrival in Ethiopia of a reported 8,000 (later 15,000) Cuban troops, however, put the shoe on the other foot. After the Somalis withdrew from the area in March 1978, the Cuban-aided Ethiopian forces appeared to pose a threat to Somalia itself, which raised the possibility of Western countermeasures.

For its part, Ethiopia's military government, which had been moving quite sharply to the left since the overthrow of Emperor Haile Selassie in 1974, has been fighting simultaneously on at least three fronts: against the Somalis in Ogaden; two separate liberation movements in the Red Sea province of Eritrea; and against insurgent terrorist opposition from both the left and the right in the nation's capital, Addis Ababa. All these divisions have spawned problems with its neighbor, Sudan, which the Dergue accuses of supporting Ethiopia's various opponents. Sudan, in term, has charged Ethiopia with complicity in several recent unsuccessful military coups. Although the two countries have recently tried to mend their rift, the potential for further conflict remains.

Sudan itself has recently shifted alignments, turning out the Soviets in March 1977 after an attempted coup said to have been fomented by Sudani Communists. Sudan is also at odds with Libya following a coup quite obviously staged with the aid of Tripoli. Sudan is now a favored aid-recipient of the conservative Arab oil powers and is firmly cementing its economic aid and military ties with the United States.

As Geoffrey Kemp emphasizes, the area is of interest to both the Soviet Union and the Western powers because of its proximity to the Middle East, as well as to Indian Ocean shipping routes. In the various conflicts on the Horn, the United States and the Western powers find themselves increasingly allied with the conservative oil powers against the Soviet Union and Libya.

In the Western Sahara conflict the role of outside powers threatens to increase. The issue here once again is territory and the antagonists face each other over something of an ideological divide. The annexation of the phosphate-rich Spanish colony of Western Sahara by Morocco and Mauritania has been violently opposed by an indigenous guerrilla movement, the Polisario, and its Algerian patron. Guerrilla terrorism against Mauritania has threatened that country's fragile political structure, and made it increasingly dependent upon the Moroccan army. The issue has been kept alive in the OAU, but the original division of the territory— and the effective abrogation of the rules of the game for colonial transfer of power to indigenous leadership—was met with some indifference. Some Soviet military aid has reportedly been channeled to the Polisario, and the French have become heavily involved in buttressing Mauritania. At French urging, the U.S. administration proposed to send "counterin-surgency" aircraft to Morocco in January 1978.

Zaire's problems with its neighbors also seem likely to continue to attract outside attention and involvement. Zaire's support of liberation movements opposed to Angola's ruling MPLA (Popular Front for the Liberation of Angola) during the civil war has created enduring antagonism between the two countries. Each now suspects the other, probably with reason, of supporting anti-government elements. Zaire accused Angola of aiding the insurgents who invaded Shaba province in spring 1977 and 1978, while Angola charged Zaire with continued harboring of the remnants of the FNLA (National Front for the Liberation of Angola) group. Here communal conflicts within the countries and ideological differences between the two governments each play a part in creating the conditions for continuing antagonism. Zaire is also at log-gerheads with neighboring Congo, and again ideological differences keep the pot boiling. Zaire sees the Soviet and Cuban aid to the Congolese military as a direct threat to its national security. Because the Western stake in Zaire is relatively high—both with regard to Zaire's copper industry, and its heavy debt [4]—Zaire's internal problems and cross-border conflicts are likely to call forth Western responses, as in the French airlift of Moroccan troops to Shaba in the spring of 1977 and the concerted Western response in May 1978.

In East Africa, the former partners in the East African Community—Kenya, Uganda, and Tanzania—maintain a state of persisting triangular political warfare. Uganda's Idi Amin has been at loggerheads with Tanzania since the latter allowed an invasion of Uganda by refugee nationals to be staged on Tanzanian territory; Ugandan hostilities with Kenya, on the other hand, threatened to erupt into armed conflict at the time of the Entebbe crisis. Tanzania and Kenya, for their part, have

[16]

allowed an ideological competition between socialism and capitalism to escalate to a point where most material ties between their countries have been summarily cut, including trade, travel, and all cross-border traffic.

The southern African conflicts have the greatest importance in international politics. There the United States and U.S.S.R. have both supported the cause of the disenfranchised black majorities in Rhodesia, Namibia, and South Africa, but possible internal settlements threaten to heighten real differences in interest between the superpowers. The transition to majority rule in the first two countries appears likely to occur by 1980. A major issue in each is the extent to which the settlement will be internationally accepted. In Rhodesia, an internal settlement between Ian Smith and black leaders inside the country, excluding the Patriotic Front and the guerrilla armies, leaves unresolved issues which may cause regional conflicts for years to come. Both the Soviet Union and the front-line states (that is, those states neighboring Rhodesia, namely, Zambia, Mozambique, Botswana, Tanzania, and Angola) have considerable interests at stake in the participation of the various liberation movements, and can support continued fighting. An internal settlement on the basis of one man-one vote universal franchise, if that settlement excludes the guerrilla fighters and is opposed by significant African states, poses exceedingly complicated political choices for the Western powers.

With regard to Namibia, the participation of the Southwest African People's Organization (SWAPO), Namibia's main liberation movement, continues to be a major bone of contention. Because SWAPO, which is made up predominantly of members of Namibia's majority tribe (the Ovambo), has the field virtually to itself, and because it has waged a successful international political campaign, its exclusion de-

[17]

prives a settlement of international legitimacy. Again, a South African turn-over of power to a group of internal leaders without SWAPO probably ensures the continuation of a guerrilla struggle.

As long as the various insurgent movements continue fighting, a pattern of cross-border warfare will pervade the region, with SWAPO attacking northern Namibia across the Angolan border, and Angola's UNITA insurgents moving in the other direction while receiving South African supplies from Namibia. On Angola's northern border with Zaire, Zairean insurgents might invade Shaba province periodically, while Zaire continues to shelter and aid anti-government Angolan insurgents. Both Mozambique and Zambia are now staging grounds for the Zimbabwean guerrillas and could continue to provide shelter and aid on some level following the exclusion of the group and leaders they have supported from a settlement. Ongoing Soviet aid to the liberation movements may also be expected if Joshua Nkomo's group (ZAPU), which has been a recipient of Soviet aid over the past decade and a half, were excluded in a settlement. On the other hand, even the inclusion of the liberation movements in an orderly transition to majority rule hardly guarantees that there will be no internal power struggles in Rhodesia and Namibia after independence. This contingency, however, does diminish the potential for external support of the parties to various conflicts.

Finally, South Africa itself constitutes a major and persisting international problem. The factors guiding U.S. policy choices in dealing with South Africa are discussed in detail by Andrew Nagorski in Chapter 6 ("U.S. Options vis-à-vis South Africa"). External support (other than moral) for the South African ANC and PAC liberation movements has hitherto been small: the liberation struggles in Rhodesia and Namibia have taken precedence, and without the support of the governments of these two countries, and Botswana, a threat to South Africa's borders cannot be mounted soon. South Africa's highly trained and well-armed military machine will in any case severely daunt would-be invaders in the foreseeable future. External aid to guerrilla and terrorist action directed against South Africa, however, will undoubtedly increase in the coming years. And unless Pretoria makes real progress toward the sharing of power with its all-black majority, internal and external economic pressures may erode the power of its white rulers.

Because the Soviet Union in all likelihood will continue to have a monopoly on military aid to the liberation movements, the Western nations and the United States will be hard put to avoid a defensive posture. The nations of black Africa will undoubtedly push the Western countries to apply political and economic sanctions against South Africa. As the pressures escalate, painful domestic divisions may be opened in the Western countries and particularly in the United States. Until a transition to a sharing in power by the black majority is achieved in South Africa, only continuing adroit diplomacy will prevent polarization along black-white, East-West, North-South lines.

NOTES

1. "U.S. Multinational Investments in Africa: The Dynamics of a Changing Relationship," by Thomas J. Biersteker. A background paper prepared for the February 23, 1977 meeting of the Council on Foreign Relations' Survey Discussion Group on U.S. Policy Toward Africa.

2. See "Black African-UN Voting Behavior on the Middle East Conflict," by Ron Kochan, Susan Aurelia Gitelson, and Ephraim

Dubek, *The Jerusalem Journal of International Relations,* Vol. I, No. 2 (Winter 1975), pp. 21-52. As the authors point out, since the resolutions were sponsored by the Arab countries, an abstention is politically unfavorable to the Arab cause. On 39 General Assembly votes from 1967 to 1972, the black African totals were; Yes—446; No—274; Abstaining or absent—425.

3.   Guinea had already broken relations in 1967.

4.   Zaire is the most heavily indebted of all black African countries, with a cumulative total of nearly $2 billion in external debt outstanding in 1977.

[ONE]

U.S. Economic Interests in Africa: Investment, Trade, and Raw Materials

Gordon Bertolin

Foreign economic activity in Africa has been dominated by the Europeans since the colonial period, with the small U.S. role confined chiefly to Liberia and South Africa. Today, however, this pattern is beginning to change. Although many of the colonial relationships remain in effect, greater global interdependence and the increasing reliance of the United States on foreign sources of oil and other raw materials have enhanced the economic importance of Africa to the United States. It is increasingly necessary, therefore, to examine American economic relations with Africa when formulating

[21]

policy toward the region. First, what are American economic interests in Africa?*

In the long run the United States has an economic interest in African economic growth, trade liberalization, and price stability. Although the global impact of these conditions in Africa is relatively small, they do contribute to the strength and stability of the international economic system and therefore are ultimately of benefit to the United States. Also of importance to the United States is the African role in the North-South dialogue concerning a new international economic order. However, these important multilateral aspects of American economic relations with Africa are discussed in Chapter 2 of this volume and will not be developed further here. What will be discussed are the more tangible, bilateral American economic interests in Africa.

The United States has, for example, several billion dollars worth of direct private investment in Africa. There is clearly an American interest in the continued ownership and profitability of these investments. In 1976 American exports to Africa totaled more than $5 billion. Continued and improved access to African markets is another American economic stake in the region. Finally, a growing proportion of American raw materials are now being provided by African nations. It is of both strategic and economic importance that these materials flow to the United States with a minimum of fluctuation in price and quantity. Therefore, it is to a description of the size and location of American investments and trade, and to an evaluation of the patterns of resource supply that the discussion now turns.

* I would like, at the outset, to thank Carol Richmond of the Council on Foreign Relations for updating the figures cited in this chapter prior to publication.

[22]

INVESTMENT

In Table 1, U.S. direct investment in Africa [1] is compared with American investment worldwide. With about $4.5 billion in direct American investment, Africa forms only a small part of the overall investment picture. That $4.5 billion represents only about 3% of all overseas direct American investment. Far more important are Europe, with 41% of the total, Canada with 25%, and Latin America with 17%. The relative unimportance of Africa in investment terms is nothing new. In percentage terms U.S. investment in Africa is now just about the same as it was in 1960, although it is down from 1970 when it was 4.5% of total overseas investment.

The largest concentration of U.S. investment in Africa is in the Republic of South Africa. In 1976, investment in South Africa was $1.66 billion, or about 37% of the total for the continent. Nigeria had another 8% of the total, as did Liberia and Libya. A complete breakdown of U.S. investment by country in Africa is not currently available,[2] but other states with large stocks of U.S. private direct investment are Zaire ($250 million), Gabon ($170 million), and Kenya ($150 million).[3]

Investment throughout the continent began in the extractive industries. Today, more than two-thirds of American direct investment in independent Africa is still in that sector. In South Africa, however, more than 50% of American investment is now in the manufacturing sector while less than 10% is in mining.[4] More significant, perhaps, than the absolute size of American investment is the growth pattern.

In recent years U.S. investment in the Republic of South Africa has been growing rapidly—92% since 1970. Over the same period U.S. investment in the rest of Africa increased

[23]

TABLE 1

U.S. Direct Private Investment Abroad
(Cumulative book value at year-end, millions of dollars)

	1950	1960	1965	1970	1975	1976
Total, all areas	11,788	32,778	49,217	78,178	124,212	137,244
Africa, total	287	925	1,904	3,482	3,996	4,467
South Africa	140	286	528	868	1,582	1,665
Other Africa	147	639	1,376	2,614	2,414	2,802
Libya	a	99	424	1,012	65	362
Liberia	16	139	201	187	334	348
Nigeria	b	b	b	b	535	341
Other	131	401	751	1,415	1,480	1,750

a Less than $500,000.
b Totals for Nigeria were included in the "Other" category until 1973.
Source: Survey of Current Business, August 1963; September 1966; November 1971; August 1977.

only 7%. However, when the substantial disinvestment in Libya is discounted, the rest of Africa shows an increase of 52% since 1970. And even this figure may underestimate the interest of American investors in the region. U.S. firms are constantly exploring and investing in petroleum and minerals. Investment is also continuing, although at a much slower pace, in the manufacturing sector. The slower growth of cumulative American investment in black Africa is due primarily to nationalizations[5] and increasing local participation.

In 1974, for example, a reduction from 1973 of $200 million in cumulative direct investment in independent Africa was entirely accounted for by a decrease in investment in Nigeria resulting from a transfer of equity from a U.S. petroleum firm to the Nigerian government. Investment in the rest of independent Africa actually increased by $26 million that

[24]

year.[6] And in the following year there was $313 million in new investment in Nigeria, followed by a drop of $194 million in 1976. The pattern which emerges is one of substantial new investments being offset as governments seek greater participation and control over business activity within their borders. The statistical result is that the percentage of total U.S. African investment in the Republic of South Africa continually increases. There are, of course, other reasons why American investment has grown more rapidly in South Africa than it has elsewhere.

The way the American investor has traditionally thought of South Africa was well expressed by John Blashill of *Fortune* magazine in 1972.

The Republic of South Africa has always been regarded by foreign investors as a gold mine, one of those rare and refreshing places where profits are great and problems small. Capital is not threatened by political instability or nationalization. Labor is cheap, the market booming, the currency hard and convertible.[7]

Some of these characteristics hold true today, others do not. For most of the last twenty-five years, returns on American investments in South Africa have been 15% and 20% (see Table 2). This figure compares very favorably with those worldwide, where returns are between 10% and 15%, and with returns in the rest of Africa which fluctuate widely. In 1975 and 1976, however, returns on investments in South Africa were lower because of the recession. Black labor is indeed cheap, but its mobility and use in skilled positions are restricted by the government and white unions, leading to artificially high wages for whites. After the Soweto riots of June 1976, one might well question how stable South Africa is.

[25]

In fact, there is some evidence that foreign investment is being curtailed. Although cumulative U.S. investment in South Africa rose by $83 million in 1976, new equity investment (as opposed to reinvested earnings) accounted for only 10% of the rise,[8] suggesting declining investor interest. Elsewhere in Africa, equity investment made up nearly two-thirds of increased investment. What is more, South Africa's reserves dropped by about a third following the riots, and they still have not recovered. However, it remains to be seen whether these developments indicate a trend or simply a pause until the situation appears more settled and the recession has passed. On balance, it would behoove the prospective investor to consider whether South Africa is really a "gold mine." Still, the government does not expropriate and historically the profits have been high. These characteristics compare very favorably, from the investor's point of view, with the rest of Africa where either the risk of nationalization is high or the profits may not be worth the effort.

The mood of the governments of most of the majority-ruled states in Africa is clearly one of preference for at least partial ownership of the means of production within their borders. Since 1960 nearly 40% of all instances of nationalization in the world have been in black Africa.[9] The transfer of equity in the petroleum industry in Nigeria was noted above. There have also been massive nationalizations in Libya, Zaire, Zambia, and Ghana.

For the most part, investors have been receiving compensation for property nationalized. This is little inducement to the investor, however, since even if he gets what he thinks his property is worth, he will lose the profits he might continue to make if he had invested his money elsewhere.

Given the possibility of nationalization and the restrictions on profit remission and business practices generally that the

[26]

TABLE 2

Earnings* on U.S. Direct Private Investment Abroad
(In millions of dollars)

	1950	1960	1965	1970	1975	1976
Total, all areas	1,766	3,566	5,431	8,789	16,434	18,843
% of investment	15.0	10.9	11.0	11.2	13.2	13.7
Africa, total	47	33	380	846	651	794
% of investment	16.4	3.6	20.0	24.3	16.3	17.8
South Africa	28	50	101	139	139	202
% of investment	20.0	17.5	19.1	16.0	8.8	12.1
Other Africa	19	−17	279	707	512	592
% of investment	12.9	−2.7	20.3	27.0	21.2	21.1
Libya	a	b	235	564	174	214
% of investment			55.4	55.7	267.7	·59.1
Liberia	15	b	17	16	53	45
% of investment	94.0		8.5	8.6	15.9	12.9
Nigeria	c	c	c	c	284	192
% of investment					53.1	56.3
Other	4	b	27	127	d	140
% of investment	3.1		3.6	9.0		8.0

* "Earnings" is the sum of the U.S. share in the net earnings of subsidiaries and branch profits.

a Not available.

b The breakdown by country is not available, but the negative earnings were completely accounted for by heavy investment in North Africa. West Africa showed earnings of 12.8%.

c Nigeria was included in the "Other" category until 1973.

d Less than $500,000 (less than 1% of investment).

Source: Survey of Current Business, December 1953; August 1962; September 1966; November 1971; August 1977.

investor will likely face, what are the inducements to invest? Earnings may be very high—in the major petroleum-producing countries, Nigeria and Libya, they have been on the order of

[27]

50% to 60%. A glance at the earnings picture elsewhere, however, shows returns which are often below 10%, and may even be much lower, as in 1975 when total earnings in Africa, not including South Africa, Nigeria, Liberia and Libya, were less than 1% of investment. The multinational corporation may have motives other than immediate profits, however.[10] Resource access in the face of dwindling domestic supplies is often one such motivation, as are access to, and control of, expanding African markets. The multinational corporation may also desire a presence in a country in order to develop an understanding of the peculiarities of that market, even though the benefits from that knowledge may be realized only in the future. Another possibility is that the corporation needs to find buyers for products that are outmoded in the home market. Finally, corporations may be lured by incentives offered by the host country.

To sum up, both multinational corporations and African governments are still in a period of probing each others' powers, limitations, capabilities, and trustworthiness, which accounts for the relatively slow growth of American investments in independent Africa. Yet the fact that investment does continue to grow is an indication that there are both governments and multinational corporations which are flexible enough to adapt to new circumstances in the pursuit of joint economic advantage.

In order to understand fully the nature of American financial involvement in Africa, two more points should be made. First, in the Republic of South Africa, 50% of all U.S. investments are owned by four firms—General Motors, Mobil, Texaco, and Ford—which happen to be four of the five largest corporations in America in terms of sales. Out of the top fifty corporations in America, twenty-nine have operations in South Africa. It is true that the investment for most of these companies amounts to less than 1% of assets, yet when considering U.S. policy in southern Africa it is instructive to remember whose investments are at stake.

TABLE 3

21 Largest Banks
U.S. Claims on Residents of Selected Foreign Countries *
(In millions of dollars)

World	66,381
Africa	1,692
Algeria	534
Egypt	177
South Africa	720
Zaire	162
Zambia	99

* As of December 31, 1975. Loans not guaranteed by EXIM bank or U.S. corporations.
Source: Hearings—Senate Foreign Relations Committee, Subcommittee on Multinational Corporations. "Multinational Banks and U.S. Foreign Policy," pp. 128-30.

The second point is that U.S. banks have considerable loan exposure in South Africa (see Table 3). At the end of 1975 that exposure amounted to nearly three-quarters of a billion dollars in loans not guaranteed by agencies of the U.S. government or by U.S. corporations.[11] Total loan exposure has been estimated at $2.2 billion.[12] As is the case with corporate investments, these loans are concentrated in a few of the largest U.S. banks. American banks do have large exposure elsewhere in Africa—$534 million in Algeria, $162 million in Zaire, and $99 million in Zambia—but no country surpasses South Africa.

To sum up, there is more U.S. investment in South Africa than in any other country on the continent, and it has been

[29]

growing rapidly. Although investments in independent Africa are substantially greater than those in South Africa, their share of the total has recently been decreasing. Finally, when considering U.S. economic interests in Africa, it should be borne in mind that so far as investments and loans are concerned, some of America's largest corporations and banks are involved.

TRADE

As is the case with investment, trade with Africa makes up only a small proportion of total U.S. foreign trade. However, with the United States facing a prolonged period of expensive energy imports, the African market is becoming increasingly important as an opportunity to redress the resulting trade deficits. Moreover, there is a growing interdependence between the African and American economies. The African nations have come to rely on our technology and agricultural goods while we are increasingly dependent on African raw materials.

In 1976, merchandise trade with Africa was nearly $18 billion, or about 7.6% of the total. In contrast, 21% of U.S. trade was with Canada, 23% with Europe, and 12% with Latin America. As recently as 1970, trade with Africa was less than $3 billion annually and made up only 3% of the total. Thus trade has grown in both absolute and relative terms. Although exports to Africa more than tripled between 1970 and 1976, the main growth in trade was due to imports which increased by more than ten times over the same period (see Table 4).

Until recently about one-third of American imports from Africa were from the Republic of South Africa. In 1976, however, only about 7% of imports came from that country.

TABLE 4

U.S. Foreign Trade
(Millions of dollars, f.a.s. value)

	1955 Exports	1955 Imports	1960 Exports	1960 Imports	1965 Exports	1965 Imports	1970 Exports	1970 Imports	1975 Exports	1975 Imports	1976 Exports	1976 Imports
World	15,518	11,382	20,500	14,654	27,346	21,366	43,226	39,963	107,591	96,140	114,997	120,677
Africa	588	619	766	535	1,224	875	1,579	1,111	4,949	8,305	5,206	12,639
South Africa	260	96	277	108	438	225	563	288	1,302	841	1,348	925
Other Africa	328	523	488	427	786	650	1,016	823	3,647	7,464	3,858	11,714
Nigeria	11	36	2	40	74	59	129	71	536	3,282	770	4,938
Algeria	13	6	24	1	21	5	62	10	632	1,359	487	2,209
Libya	4	a	42	a	64	31	104	39	232	1,046	277	2,243
Angola	12	32	1	25	13	48	38	68	53	426	35	264
Egypt	78	25	150	31	158	16	81	23	683	28	810	93
Gabon	b	b	b	b	5	10	7	9	59	197	46	190
Ghana	7	50	26	53	36	59	59	91	100	150	133	155
Ivory Coast	b	b	b	b	11	46	36	92	78	160	64	248
Zaire	b	b	b	b	70	38	62	41	188	67	99	189

a Less than $50,000.
b Data not given separately.

Sources: *U.S. Foreign Trade: Import Trade by Country,* January 1956; January 1961; December 1965.
  U.S. Foreign Trade: Export Trade by Country, January 1956; January 1961; December 1965.
  Highlights of U.S. Export-Import Trade, December 1970; December 1975; December 1976.

Although imports from South Africa have tripled since 1970, imports from five energy producers—Gabon, Algeria, Nigeria, Libya, and Angola—have increased by an incredible 5,000%. In 1976, about 40% of all American imports from Africa came from Nigeria alone. Much of this increase is due to the rise in the price of oil, but it also reflects the emergence of Africa as a major supplier of energy to the United States.

American imports from Africa are almost exclusively raw materials. Besides petroleum, the United States imports several important minerals from Africa as well as various agricultural commodities. The economic importance of the mineral imports will be discussed in the section on raw materials.

South Africa has always been America's best customer in Africa. That country still spends $500 million more on U.S. goods than the next best customer on the continent, Egypt, but others are gaining quickly. Since 1970, exports to South Africa have grown only half as fast as exports to the rest of the continent. And in 1976, U.S. exports to South Africa increased only 1% while exports to Nigeria increased by 44%.

U.S. exports to independent Africa include food, capital goods such as mining and construction machinery, and manufactured goods, especially aircraft, locomotives and cars. Exports to South Africa cover a very wide spectrum, but especially important to that country have been the computers, communications equipment, and aircraft it has purchased from the United States.[13]

Imports from Africa outnumber exports by more than two to one. Thus the United States has a sizeable trade deficit with the continent as a whole (see Table 5). The trading patterns are such, however, that the United States has a large trade surplus with South Africa, nearly half a billion dollars. This leaves a trade deficit with the rest of the continent of almost $8 billion.

[32]

TABLE 5

Balance of Trade
(Millions of dollars)

	1955	1960	1965	1970	1975	1976
World	4,136	5,845	5,980	3,263	11,451	−5,680
Africa	−31	230	349	469	−3,355	−7,433
South Africa	164	169	213	275	462	423
Other Africa	−196	61	136	194	−3,817	−7,856
Nigeria	−25	−37	16	57	−2,745	−4,168
Algeria	7	23	15	52	−727	−1,722
Libya	4	42	33	65	−814	−1,966
Angola	−20	−24	−35	−30	−373	−229
Egypt	53	119	142	58	655	717
Gabon	a	a	−5	−2	−138	−144
Ghana	−43	−26	−23	−32	−50	−22
Ivory Coast	a	a	−35	−56	−82	−184
Zaire	a	a	32	21	121	−90

a Data not given separately.

Sources: *U.S. Foreign Trade: Import Trade by Country,* January 1956;
January 1961; December 1965.
U.S. Foreign Trade: Export Trade by Country, January 1956;
January 1961; December 1965.
Highlights of U.S. Export–Import Trade, December 1970;
December 1975; December 1976.

Some writers have pointed to the trade surplus with South Africa as a major economic interest in the area.[14] There can be no doubt that this trade surplus is beneficial to the U.S. balance-of-payments situation, but it does not necessarily follow that the chief trading interest is in South Africa. If the U.S. goal is to improve the balance-of-trade situation in Africa, it hardly seems likely that this can be achieved through an increase in exports to South Africa. That country already has a

[33]

large trade deficit with the United States and has recently experienced a diminution of its foreign exchange reserves.[15]

A more promising avenue for improving the balance of trade would seem to be to try to increase exports to those countries which currently have large trade surpluses with the United States and consequently have the dollars with which to buy American goods. Another reason for suspecting that the future growth of U.S. exports to Africa will come in the majority-ruled states is that the economies, and therefore imports, of the energy producers are growing far more rapidly than is the economy of recession-troubled South Africa. Although the U.S. market share is growing in many countries, it is typically less than 15%, well behind European competitors.[16] Thus considerable opportunity for expansion exists as African leaders try to reduce their dependence on former metropolitan powers for trading relations. One step in this direction was taken when the reverse tariff preferences which had been granted to the Europeans by many African countries were eliminated as part of the Lomé agreement.[17]

To sum up, at present U.S. imports from Africa come primarily from the energy producers among the independent states. South Africa is America's best customer, but others are gaining ground. Both imports and exports are concentrated in a few countries, with more than 85% of the trade taking place between the United States and only ten countries. The United States currently has a large trade surplus with South Africa and a deficit with the rest of Africa as a whole. Finally, prospects for increasing trade seem to lie primarily with the energy producers.

RAW MATERIALS

During periods of raw materials shortages one often hears predictions of the impending exhaustion of the world's mineral resources. The period since the Arab oil embargo of 1973 has been no exception. Although the recession of 1974-75 cooled demand for raw materials and some recent observers [18] seem to feel that the actual physical resources of vital raw materials are adequate for many years to come, the financial, managerial and political requirements for their successful exploitation leave the adequacy of future productive capacity in doubt. An extended period of tight supply conditions remains a real possibility. Such a period, with its attendant fluctuations in prices and supplies of raw materials, can cause serious economic and political difficulties even for a nation as relatively well supplied with its own resources as the United States.

Interruption of supplies and/or wide price swings can wreak havoc with industry planning and necessitate the maintenance of costly and unproductive stockpiles. What is more, even if the price of a material comes down after a period of shortage, the inflationary impact will persist since the prices of manufactured goods tend to be "sticky" in a downward direction. Because of the long lead-times involved in developing new sources of mineral supply, or even increasing the capacity of old sources, it is difficult to change traditional supply patterns, even when political or economic advantage would suggest such a change. At the international level, the more vulnerable Western European and Japanese economies are closely tied to our own, making any threat to their raw materials supplies an indirect threat to our own economy. Finally, international competition for scarce resources could lead developed nations to seek independent solutions, thus endangering traditional friendships. Therefore the United States has a substantial economic and political interest in the steady growth of productive capacity, in the stability of raw materials prices, and in the protection of delivery systems worldwide. The purpose of this discussion, however, is to focus specifically on the U.S. dependence on African sources of raw materials.

In a 1974 study by the Council on International Economic Policy,[19] independent African nations were shown to be relatively unimportant suppliers of critical imported non-fuel materials. Of twenty materials examined, independent Africa provides more than 10% of American import needs for just four. Canada is the major supplier, filling 50% of American needs. The bulk of the remainder is provided by other Western hemisphere countries, Australia, and the Republic of South Africa. These results were viewed with relative equanimity by the CIEP since, in its opinion, "Canada, Australia or South Africa would be unlikely to participate in any embargo of exports to the United States. . . ."[20] It should be noted that although these nations are unlikely to support a politically motivated embargo, all raw materials producers are becoming more aggressive in their dealings with consumers. If fuels are included in the analysis, however, the importance of independent Africa is enhanced. African nations now supply the United States with fully one-third of all its imported crude petroleum.

In order to evaluate U.S. dependence on raw materials imported from all of Africa, eleven materials—including chromium, cobalt, manganese, bauxite, antinomy, columbium, vanadium, platinum, gold, petroleum, and uranium—will be examined. Ten of these, including seven from the CIEP study, are commodities for which the United States must rely on

TABLE 6

African Production and Resources of Certain Raw Materials

Mineral	% of World Production (1974)	% of World Resources [a]
Antimony	South Africa (22%); Morocco (3%)	South Africa (6%)
Bauxite	Guinea (8%); Other (1%)	Guinea (26%); Cameroon (4%); Ghana (2%) [b]
Chromium	South Africa (26%); Rhodesia (8%); Madagascar (2%)	South Africa (71%); Rhodesia (26%)
Cobalt	Zaire (58%); Zambia (10%); Morocco (6%)	Zaire (18%); Zambia (8%)
Columbium	Nigeria (6%)	Zaire (3%); Kenya (3%); Uganda (2%); Nigeria (2%); Other (2%) [b]
Gold	South Africa (61%); Ghana (2%)	South Africa (53%)
Manganese	South Africa (17%); Gabon (10%); Other (4%)	South Africa (42%); Gabon (2%)
Petroleum	Nigeria (4%); Libya (3%); Algeria (2%); Other (1%)	Libya (4%); Nigeria (2%); Algeria (2%); Other (1%) [b]
Platinum	South Africa (45%)	South Africa (47%)
Uranium	South Africa (14%); Niger (5%); Gabon (3%)	South Africa (16%) [c]; Niger (2%); Other (2%) [d]
Vanadium	South Africa (46%)	South Africa (32%) [c]

[a] Resources are known deposits whether economical or not at current prices and technology. Reserves are that portion of resources recoverable under present conditions.

[b] Reserves only.

[c] Production and resource figures for South Africa include Namibia (Southwest Africa).

[d] Figures exclude U.S.S.R.

Sources: U.S. Department of the Interior, Bureau of Mines, *Minerals Yearbook, 1974.*
U.S. Department of the Interior, Bureau of Mines, *Mineral Facts and Problems, 1975.*
U.S. Geological Survey *Professional Papers 817 & 820.*

[37]

imports for more than 35% of consumption and for which African nations are major suppliers.[21] The eleventh, uranium, is potentially an important African import.

Before beginning the analysis of individual commodities, a few points need to be mentioned. First, there are many major raw materials which do not fall within the purview of this discussion. Among them are: iron, copper, coal, tungsten, tin, and nickel. In fact, in terms of overall raw materials availability, the United States is in a rather enviable position. Of the materials examined by the CIEP, it was found that the United States depended on imports for only 15% of its consumption. This figure compares very favorably with those for Europe and Japan which were 75% and 90%, respectively. Second, for the purposes of this discussion, "resources" are defined as known mineral deposits whether or not they are recoverable given existing prices and technology. "Reserves" are that portion of resources which are recoverable under present conditions. Information on U.S. stockpiles of the various minerals is included to illustrate American preparedness to deal with a cut-off of supplies. However, under current law these stockpiles can only be used during a national emergency and are therefore of no value in combating economic dislocations caused by a lack of capacity or fluctuating prices. Figures cited refer to Tables 6, 7, 8 and 9.[22]

Uses and Sources of Chief Minerals Imported from Africa

Chromium

Chromium is essential in the manufacture of stainless steel and is also used as a chemical and to make refractory bricks. There are no satisfactory substitutes for chromium. The United States mines no chromium of its own and is 91% dependent on imports for its

TABLE 7

U.S. Import Dependence on Certain Raw Materials

Mineral	Percentage Imported [a]	Major African Sources [b]
Columbium	100	Nigeria (10%)
Manganese	99	Gabon (32%); South Africa (12%)
Cobalt	98	Zaire (37%) [c]
Chromium	91	South Africa (24%); Rhodesia (12%)
Bauxite	85	Guinea (16%)
Platinum group metals	80	South Africa (68%) [d]
Antimony	56	South Africa (22%)
Gold	45	NA
Vanadium	36	South Africa (59%)
Petroleum	35	Nigeria (17%); Algeria (7%); Libya (6%)

[a] *Source: Minerals and Materials: a Monthly Survey;* U.S. Bureau of Mines–September, 1976; 1975 figures.

[b] *Source: U.S. Imports for Consumption and General Imports;* U.S. Department of Commerce; 1975 figures; "major" is defined as greater than 5%.

[c] Another 22% comes from Belgium, the major original source of which is Zaire.

[d] Another 27% comes from Great Britain, the major original source of which is South Africa.

NA—Not available.

supplies, the rest coming from stockpiles and secondary recovery. In 1975 the United States imported 24% of its chromium from the Republic of South Africa and another 12% from Rhodesia. The rest came from the U.S.S.R., Turkey, and the Philippines. With the repeal of the Byrd amendment the United States will no longer import chromium from Rhodesia.

The world's resources of chromium are large, with reserves alone estimated to be sufficient for more than 100 years. However, they are highly concentrated. 97% of identified resources are in Rhodesia and South Africa. Productive capacity is more diversified than resources, with only about one-third in southern Africa. With no known reserves of chromium, the United States will remain totally dependent on foreign sources for this crucial material. Reflecting the

[39]

TABLE 8

Domestic Primary Production as a Percentage of
Primary Demand for Certain Raw Materials

Mineral	1955	1965	1970	1974	1985	2000
Antimony	14%	10%	12%	6%	5%	5%
Bauxite	26	13	13	8	6	10
Chromium	9	0	0	0	0	0
Cobalt	25	8	4	0	48*	93*
Columbium	1	0	0	0	0	0
Gold	142	32	29	29	18	14
Manganese	21	6	5	2	2	0
Petroleum	89	78	77	63	44	27
Platinum	3	3	2	1	1	1
Uranium	1180	1754	274	122	88	86
Vanadium	194	85	79	64	59	26

* Figure includes projected supplies from the seabed.
Source: Mineral Facts and Problems–1975; Figures for 1985 and
2000 are forecasts of what the Bureau of Mines thinks will
happen rather than simply extensions of current trends.

importance of chromium, government and private stocks are sufficient to meet nearly three years consumption at 1974 levels.

Cobalt

Cobalt is used as an alloying element in the production of high
strength and high temperature alloys, as well as in magnets. For
some uses nickel may be substituted for cobalt. The United States
currently produces no cobalt and is consequently 98% dependent on
imports for its supply. In 1975 the United States imported 37% of its
cobalt from Zaire and another 22% from Belgium, whose major
original source was Zaire. Other U.S. sources were Finland, Norway
and Canada.

TABLE 9

Stockpile Inventories for Selected Commodities

Commodity	Months' Consumption in U.S. Govt. Stockpiles	Months' Consumption in U.S. Private Stocks
Antimony	*	8
Bauxite	7	3
Chromium	26	8
Cobalt	30	1
Columbium	4	7
Manganese	39	20
Petroleum	*	2
Platinum	10	6
Uranium	*	31
Vanadium	1	4

Note: Stockpile levels are for December, 1975, except antimony and uranium (12/74) and petroleum (12/76). Months' consumption was calculated using 1974 consumption levels, since they represent peak usage in recent years.

* No strategic stockpile.

Sources: CBO, *U.S. Raw Materials Policy: Problems and Possible Solutions,* p. 38.

U.S. Bureau of Mines, *Minerals & Materials: a Monthly Survey,* May, 1977.

U.S. Bureau of Mines, *Minerals Yearbook, 1974.*

The world's reserves are at present considered to be sufficient for almost 90 years. 23% of the world's reserves are in Zaire and Zambia. The United States has 18% of the world's resources, but they are at present uneconomical to mine. Although production of cobalt is now highly concentrated, supply will diversify if the deep-sea nodules, which contain significant quantities of cobalt, prove economically and politically feasible to recover. A price rise would greatly contribute to U.S. self-sufficiency by facilitating deep-sea mining and by drawing forth presently uneconomical U.S. resources. Given

[41]

such a price rise and a favorable outcome at the Law of the Sea conferences, the United States should be nearly self-sufficient in cobalt by the year 2000. Stocks are currently sufficient for 25 years' usage.

Manganese

Manganese is crucial to the production of steel, which is brittle without it. There are no satisfactory substitutes. The United States mines no manganese and is dependent on imports for 99% of its supply since secondary recovery is negligible. In 1975 it imported 32% of its manganese from Gabon and another 12% from South Africa. Brazil was the other major supplier.

World resources of manganese are highly concentrated with 42% in South Africa and another 42% in the Soviet Union. Production is nearly as concentrated, with 75% being produced by four countries— U.S.S.R., South Africa, Brazil, and Gabon. Although Gabon is currently an important producer of manganese, it has less than 2% of the world's resources. World reserves are considered to be sufficient for 60 years. As is the case with cobalt, manganese is recoverable from deep-sea nodules. Thus future world supply may be diversified. Without exploitation of sea-bed resources, the United States will remain almost totally dependent on imports for its supply of manganese. Both government and private stocks are large and together can meet six years' consumption.

Bauxite

Demand for aluminum metal, which is produced from bauxite, has been growing rapidly for many years and the use of aluminum now exceeds that of all other metals except iron. Aluminum is used in virtually all segments of the world economy, including construction, transportation, communications, packaging, consumer durables, and

[42]

defense applications. At higher prices other aluminum-bearing ores become competitive with bauxite. The United States imports about 85% of its bauxite and has reserves sufficient to meet only two to three years' consumption. The United States meets about 5% of its demand from old scrap. Guinea supplies the United States with about 16% of its imports. Other foreign sources are Jamaica, Australia, Surinam, and Canada.

Known reserves of bauxite are sufficient to meet world demand beyond the year 2000. Africa currently produces about 10% of the world's bauxite, primarily in Guinea. As infrastructure is developed to reach known deposits, Africa will become a more important supplier since it has nearly one-third of the world's resources of bauxite. The United States is expected to remain heavily dependent on foreign sources. Stockpiles are sufficient to meet about 10 months' usage.

Antimony

The major use of antimony is in the manufacture of storage and car batteries, although it is also used in the production of ammunition components. Other metals can be substituted for some applications. The United States depends on imports for 95% of its primary antimony, but for only 56% of the total since substantial secondary recovery is possible. 22% of America's imported antimony came from South Africa in 1975, with other major sources being China, Mexico and Bolivia.

World resources of antimony are large and should be sufficient, considering recycling possibilities, but 70% of the world's resources are in China. South Africa currently produces 25% of the world's antimony but has only 5% of the resources. Africa has no other significant resources of antimony. No significant change in U.S. dependence is expected. There are no strategic stocks of antimony, but private stocks can meet eight months' demand.

[43]

Columbium and Vanadium

These two minerals are used primarily as alloying elements in the production of steel. They can be substituted for one another and are both replaceable with molybdenum, titanium, tungsten, or tantulum, depending on the use. The United States is currently totally dependent on foreign sources for columbium and 36% dependent for vanadium. The United States imports 10% of its columbium from Nigeria and 59% of its vanadium from the Republic of South Africa. Brazil and Canada are the other major sources of columbium, and Chile is the other major foreign source of vanadium.

Reserves of both minerals are estimated to be sufficient for more than 50 years. 18% of the world's reserves of columbium are in Nigeria, Kenya, Uganda and Zaire, although these countries currently only produce 5% of the world's columbium. The major producer is Brazil with 75% of the total. 20% of the world's reserves of vanadium are in South Africa and another 70% are in the Soviet Union. Those two countries account for two-thirds of the world's vanadium production. The United States will remain totally dependent in columbium and become increasingly so in vanadium. Reflecting the numerous potential substitutes for columbium and vanadium, stocks are sufficient for only 12 and 4 months', respectively.

Platinum group metals

The six metals in this group, all of which are readily substituted for one another, have a wide variety of uses in the chemical, petroleum and electronics industries. They are also used in dentistry, jewelry and in the emission control devices of all new automobiles in the United States. Virtually no platinum is mined domestically, so that the country is 80% dependent on imports for its supplies. The major foreign supplier is South Africa with 68% of the total. The

[44]

other major source is Britain, which gets most of its platinum from South Africa and the U.S.S.R.

Both the production and resources of platinum metals are highly concentrated, with about 47% of the total in South Africa and the same in the Soviet Union. Platinum can be recovered from secondary sources with little loss, but the United States will continue to be dependent on foreign sources for primary platinum. Stockpiles can meet 16 months' demand.

Gold

Gold has a wide variety of industrial uses as well as its more obvious roles in jewelry and as a monetary reserve. Although the role of gold in the international monetary system has been reduced since the creation of SDRs and the abandonment of the two-tier pricing system, it persists as a major influencing factor in all international monetary developments. Thus the United States has a clear interest in the orderly production and marketing of gold.

The United States depends on imports for 45% of its gold. Patterns of trade are difficult to evaluate because of the movement of newly mined gold through Zurich and London, and because of monetary movement between central banks. Since about two-thirds of world gold production is in South Africa, that country is clearly a major source of new gold for the United States.

A little more than half the world's resources of gold are in South Africa, which means that an increasing proportion of the world's new gold will come from other sources, notably the Soviet Union. U.S. domestic production is expected to supply only 14% of domestic requirements by the year 2000.

Petroleum

The economic and strategic importance of petroleum is well known and needs no elaboration here. The U.S. import dependence

[45]

was about 35% in 1975 and is continually increasing. In 1975, 17% of American petroleum imports came from Nigeria, a crucial source of supply during the Arab oil embargo. Altogether about one-third of U.S. petroleum imports come from Africa. Besides Nigeria, the important suppliers of oil and natural gas are Gabon, Angola, Libya and Algeria.

Even with the addition of all the oil from Alaska, it is unlikely that the United States will be able to reduce its dependence on foreign oil. In fact, the United States is expected to supply only about one-fourth of its own petroleum by the year 2000. Therefore Africa, with its 10% of the world's reserves of petroleum, will remain an important source of supply. At present there is no strategic stockpile of petroleum, and private stocks were sufficient to meet only two months' consumption at the end of 1976. However, the Energy Policy and Conservation Act of 1975 mandated the creation of a U.S. strategic petroleum reserve of 150 million barrels (9 days' consumption) by December 1978, and 500 million barrels (29 days consumption) by December 1982.[23]

Uranium

At the present time the United States is the world's largest producer of uranium, accounting for about half the production outside the Soviet Union. Domestic sources should be sufficient to meet demand until the 1990s. By that time the level of demand, and of dependence, will depend on developments in the nuclear energy field, which are now difficult to predict.

World resources outside the Soviet Union are concentrated in the United States, Sweden, Canada, Australia, and South Africa. They are considered to be sufficient to meet world demand only until the late 1980s. Uranium resources in the centrally planned economies are not reported, although they are generally assumed to be quite large. The South African share of world resources is 16%, including those of Namibia which now has the world's largest uranium mine. Another 5% of world resources are in the Central African Empire,

Gabon, and Niger. If the world turns to nuclear power to meet its energy needs, these African resources could be crucial.

From the preceding discussion it should be clear that Africa, and South Africa in particular, is a major supplier of a number of the minerals for which the United States is highly dependent on imports. Perhaps more significantly, for six of these minerals—gold, platinum, manganese, antimony, vanadium, and chromium—more than two-thirds of the world's resources are concentrated in the white-ruled states of southern Africa and either the Soviet Union or China. Not surprisingly, U.S. stockpiles of three of the most crucial of these—platinum, manganese, and chromium—average three years' supply. In its report on critical imported materials the CIEP admitted that some cartel-type action was possible owing to the high concentration of resources. It did not consider this possibility to be a serious one, however, because, in the case of chromium, "the current political polarization among chromite producers makes the possibility of sustained cartel-like action . . . remote." [24] Some of the confidence with which the CIEP viewed the raw materials picture might well disappear if the regime in South Africa were to change. However, the dangers of such a change should not be exaggerated.

In the first place, none of the materials discussed above compares in importance to petroleum in terms of either its impact on the price structure or its centrality to the economic process. Second, for a cartel to be successful, some producers must be willing to cut back on production. Saudi Arabia could easily afford to take on this role in OPEC, but it is unclear who would be willing or able to bear this burden in prospective minerals cartels. Furthermore, with the appropriate changes in the legislation regarding stockpiles, the substan-

[47]

tial American stocks of the most crucial minerals could be used to combat cartels. The potential for market collusion remains, but would future South African governments act substantially differently from the present one in terms of a minerals policy?

It goes without saying that the present South African government is unlikely to collude openly with either the Soviet Union or the developing countries to raise raw materials prices. However, the possibility that South Africa might raise prices and restrict supply unilaterally, with other producers cooperating tacitly, should not be ruled out. In fact, just such an arrangement is in operation now in the diamonds market. It is open to question, then, just how much more market power a different South African government would be able to exercise. In any case the United States should attempt to diversify its sources of raw materials. Too great a concentration of suppliers, even if they are friendly, is unsound economically and perhaps politically. Independent Africa with its many undeveloped resources and less thoroughly surveyed territories provides an excellent opportunity for such diversification.

A final point worth noting is the potential importance of the deep-sea nodules. Both cobalt and manganese, for which the United States is more than 90% dependent, and copper, for which it is increasingly dependent, are obtainable from this source. Thus, the future raw materials importance of several African nations to the United States will be greatly affected by developments in the technology of deep-sea mining and at the Law of the Sea conferences.

Conclusions

Let it be stated at the outset that the evidence presented suggests very strongly that economic interests should be given a rather low priority in the overall policy evaluation. The trade and investment figures, although large in absolute terms, are small relative to global American activity. Europe, Canada, and Latin America are all far more important to the United States economically. Even the crucial raw materials which come from Africa are relatively few in number, although this aspect will have to be given greater weight. In Africa, then, none of these economic factors should play a determining role in political decision-making for the United States.

This is not to say that economic considerations have no role to play whatsoever. Concern about Zaire's international debt position and for the substantial American investments there probably did bear upon the U.S. response to the rebellions in Shaba province, but it was subordinate to political and strategic considerations. Simiarly, the American economic interest in the Angolan civil war argued for a quick settlement so that Gulf could resume production of Cabindan oil. Yet American policy was clearly not motivated by this consideration. In most African crises, as in these two cases, American economic interests cannot be ignored completely, but due to their relative unimportance they are unlikely to be the deciding factor. Only in the cases of Nigeria's oil and South Africa's minerals do the facts suggest that vital American economic interests might play a determining role in American policy formulation.

It should be clear from the figures presented on trade, investment, and raw materials that independent Africa easily outstrips South Africa in economic importance to the United States, and the dominant economic force of independent Africa is Nigeria. Nigeria's GNP is fast approaching that of South Africa and with its much faster growth rate should surpass it in 1978. There is twice as much trade between the United States and Nigeria as there is between this country and

South Africa, and Nigeria is at least as important as a source of raw materials. Furthermore, even though there was only one-quarter as much investment in Nigeria as in South Africa in 1976, those investments earned nearly as much. Yet does this increasing economic stake imply any Nigerian influence over our Africa policy? Do our economic interests in Nigeria and other independent African states in any way constrain American policy choices vis-à-vis South Africa?

Most American economic goals concerning trade promotion, investment protection, and reliable production and supply of raw materials can best be served by promoting cordial political relations with African governments. These efforts will, however, be dominated by our policy toward South Africa. So long as the American position on South Africa is perceived as backward by Africans, the resulting suspicions and hostilities may prove detrimental to American business interests. On the other hand, the impact of any such changes in attitude toward Americans would probably be marginal. Certainly no vital interests are involved.

More serious is the possibility that Nigeria, perhaps in conjunction with other African oil exporters, would attempt to use oil leverage to influence U.S. policy, even at some economic cost to themselves. Other African nations have voluntarily undergone substantial economic hardship in the interest of achieving majority rule in southern Africa. Some potential for leverage certainly exists as Nigeria is America's second largest external supplier of crude petroleum. But it seems unlikely that the United States could actually be forced to change its position in a direct confrontation, unless the African effort coincided with another Arab oil embargo. Even if Nigeria could influence the United States in this way, it is hardly likely that it would actually turn off the oil. With ambitious development plans which are going to be difficult to achieve in any case, Nigeria can ill afford to forego its major source of revenue.

The weakness of any direct linkages between political and economic relations was demonstrated by the attitudes of both the United States and Nigeria during the Angolan civil war. With the United States and Nigeria supporting opposed factions in that struggle, political relations became strained. Yet the active role of American businessmen in Nigeria and the flow of Nigerian oil to the United States continued unabated. Neither country's political behavior was constrained by the economic relationship, and business was unhindered by the political chill.

Regarding South Africa, our stake there—$1.66 billion in investments, $200 million in annual profits, $2.2 billion in loans outstanding, a half billion dollar balance-of-trade surplus, and significant supplies of several vital raw materials—has already been described. But that description doesn't indicate what course of action would best protect those interests, or even what the economic costs of a particular course of action are likely to be. Because the future political situation in South Africa is likely to be quite different from that which prevails at present, the role and impact of American economic interests in South Africa will be examined in the short and long run, as well as during a possible transition period.

In the very short term, American economic interests would benefit most from a continuation of the status quo. Although new investors may be losing interest in South Africa and American banks are increasingly reluctant to extend loans to the South African government,[25] the American investments already in place continue to earn profits and, more importantly, the raw materials continue to flow regularly. On the other hand, although American economic interests may be benefited in the short run by exploitation of current condi-

[51]

tions, American policy options are not seriously constrained by the economic realities.

The United States could, for example, impose political or economic sanctions against South Africa with little or no danger to vital economic interests, although there would be economic costs. If the United States stepped up its political campaign against South Africa, presumably through the U.N. framework, the South African government would be hard put to retaliate through economic means, such as a minerals embargo. It needs the foreign exchange provided by its minerals exports to the West to finance the imports of capital and technology necessary for continued economic growth, and it has nowhere else to turn. An American prohibition on new investments and loans would of course deny Americans those generally lucrative opportunities, but other outlets for American capital are readily available. Withdrawal of current investments would be more difficult because the South African government has developed the apparatus to block the outflow of capital, although the same result could be achieved eventually by not replacing depreciated investments. Strict economic sanctions of the sort proposed by Andrew Nagorski in Chapter 6 would be most difficult because imports of South African raw materials would have to be foregone. Although alternative sources of supply can be developed in time, an abrupt decision to prohibit imports of South African minerals could dislocate some areas of various Western economies. This damage might be reduced by resort to strategic stockpiles to fill the void, although these are, and probably should be, restricted to other uses.

With regard to South Africa, however, a policy founded on a projection of short-term conditions is both unrealistic and unwise. Although it is impossible to predict the time or nature of change, there can be little doubt that fundamental changes are in the offing. Policy formulation must therefore take into account the probable nature of a governing configuration in the future as well as the likely impact of the period of transition, which may be the most economically salient aspect of the entire problem. Of the many potential political outcomes in South Africa—partition, coalition, federalism, "moderate" black rule, "radical" black rule—only the last excites fears for American economic interests in the area. In fact, some writers [26] have pointed to the likely consequences of a radical black government coming to power as a compelling reason to support the present government.

Some of the economic threats a militant black government would pose are undeniable. To the extent that continued American economic involvement in South Africa prolongs the life of the present regime, future governments may be prejudiced against Western business participation in the South African economy. American investments and loans would certainly be endangered, although even a radical government might be restrained by hopes of doing business with the West in the future. Even if the investments and loans were lost entirely, however, it would not be a catastrophic blow to the American economy. Most of the corporations which operate in South Africa have less than 1% of their assets there. Although their loss would be detrimental, they are not vital to the health of the national economy, and American policy should not be based on this contingency. More serious is the question of commodity supply.

According to Hahn and Cottrell, "the Soviet Union . . . aims at manipulating the supply of these commodities [South African minerals] to Western markets." [27] The argument is that by denying the West access to South African minerals a drastic jolt would be given to Western economies, alliances would crumble as developed nations competed for resources, and cartelization would run rampant. In Chapter 4 Geoffrey Kemp has also suggested that a new government under Soviet influence might flood the gold market in an attempt to disrupt Western financial systems. Although the danger to Western economies is somewhat overstated in this analysis, it is clear that a cut-off of South African minerals would be disruptive, perhaps seriously so. Two different situations are being hypothesized here—one, that an embargo will be imposed for political or strategic reasons, and the other, that cartels will be formed to raise prices.

Concerning an embargo, the first problem is the assumption that groups which have been assisted by Moscow will be subservient to Russian dictates. It should be obvious from the flip-flop on the Horn of African, if not from previous African history, that no African alliances should be considered permanent. African leaders are primarily nationalistic, wherever they get their weapons. Even if the new government were to remain sympathetic to the Soviet Union, which is plausible in the short run, is it really likely that it could be induced to act against its own national interest to further Soviet goals? A new South African government is going to be just as anxious to sell its raw materials abroad as the present one, especially if it is more interested in promoting the welfare of all its people. Radical governments in Guinea and Angola have been far from reticent about providing the West with bauxite and petroleum. If there is an embargo enforced by Soviet arms, this would presumably call into play our strategic stockpiles, which are more than sufficient in the commodities concerned. Therefore there would seem to be little threat from a Soviet attempt at an outright embargo.

Cartelization is a more realistic possibility since the cooperation required would be in the national economic interest rather than against it. Because of the concentration of some minerals in South Africa, some form of market manipulation is in the national interest, whatever the ideological stripe of the government. But even though a successful cartel would clearly be beneficial to both South Africa and the Soviet Union, there are difficulties in achieving and maintaining one. The major problem South Africa would face is the loss of employment in the mining industry that would be caused by the supply restrictions necessary to raise prices. And even if a cartel is successful, it carries the seeds of its own destruction as higher prices encourage cheating on production agreements and greater production elsewhere in the world. Finally, even a successful doubling or tripling of the prices of the few commodities in question would not have nearly the economic impact of the rise in oil prices.

One area sometimes overlooked in the discussion of American economic interests in South Africa is the impact the transition from the present status quo to a future political entity might have. If, as seems increasingly likely, South Africa's future holds a period of prolonged and violent struggle, the economic repercussions for the United States could be quite damaging. In an environment of increasing violence the economic costs to the United States would begin to mount. American-owned property would certainly be vulnerable to attack. A war-ravaged economy could scarcely be expected to yield normal profits and trading patterns would be disrupted. The strain of war on the South African economy would be detrimental to American exports, assuming that the United States was not selling arms to the South Africans. But most dangerous would be the impact on raw materials supply. As the disruption of these supplies would be both unpredictable and uncontrollable, prices would skyrocket and physical shortages would occur, with the adverse economic and political consequences in the West described earlier.

[55]

The implications of American economic interests in Africa for our overall Africa policy are readily apparent. First, although increased cooperation with the majority-ruled states, and particularly with the energy producers, would probably bring some economic advantage to the United States, our economic stake in those states does not dictate a particular policy with regard to South Africa. In South Africa itself, there are short-run economic benefits under a continuation of the present system. However, vital American economic interests are compatible with all peaceful results, so that there is no compelling economic reason why the United States should support the present regime.

There appears to be no overriding reason why new investments in and exports to South Africa couldn't be halted if our other interests indicated that course, but it would be difficult for the United States to adhere immediately to U.N. sanctions regarding the import of South African minerals. The United States ought, therefore, to be cautious about agreeing to sanctions against South Africa until it determines where the alternate supplies are to be obtained. In order to free the United States from this constraint on its policy options, alternate supplies of the most vital materials should be developed as quickly as possible.

Finally, the economic worst case would seem to be a prolonged and chaotic war in South Africa, in which markets for vital materials would be disrupted with uncertain prospects for the restoration of supplies. Since a continuation of the present South African government without widespread violence and economic chaos seems an unlikely prospect, American support for peaceful change to a more representative system, whatever its ideological bent, would best protect long-run American economic interests in South Africa.

NOTES

1. The Department of Commerce, from which much information was drawn, includes the countries of North Africa in its definition of Africa. To be consistent this paper will do the same.

2. In annual reports of the *Survey of Current Business* on overseas private direct investment, data are given only for South Africa, Libya, Nigeria, and Liberia.

3. U.S. Department of Commerce, *Overseas Business Report,* "Market Profiles for Africa" (Washington, D.C.: Government Printing Office), December 1976.

4. Barbara Rogers, *White Wealth and Black Poverty: American Investments in Southern Africa* (Westport, Conn.: Greenwood Press, 1976), p. 125.

5. "Nationalization" is defined here as all takings of foreign investments by a government, including takings which are partial and compensated. See Leslie L. Rood, "Nationalization and Indigenization in Africa," *Journal of Modern African Studies,* vol. 14, no. 3 (1976), p. 429.

6. William Schaufele, "U.S. Economic Relations with Africa," Speech before the African-American Chamber of Commerce, New York, N.Y., February 18, 1976, p. 2, reprinted in a Department of State News Release.

7. John Blashill, "The Proper Role of U.S. Corporations in South Africa," *Fortune,* July 1972, p. 49.

8. U.S. Senate, Committee on Foreign Relations, Subcommittee on African Affairs, "U.S. Corporate Interests in Africa," January 1978, p. 8.

9. Leslie L. Rood, *op. cit.*, p. 431.

10. The author is indebted to Thomas Bierstecker for his discussion of the motivations of multinational corporations in "U.S. Multinational Investments in Africa: A Changing Relationship," Background paper no. 4 for the Council on Foreign Relations Study Group on U.S. Policy Toward Africa, February 23, 1977.

11. U.S. Senate, Hearings, Committee on Foreign Relations, Subcommittee on Multinational Corporations, "Multinational Banks and U.S. Foreign Policy," 1976, p. 128-30.

12. U.S. Senate, Committe on Foreign Relations, Subcommittee on African Affairs, "U.S. Corporate Interests in Africa," January 1978, p. 7.

13. Mohamed A. El-Khawas and Barry Cohen, eds., *The Kissinger Study of Southern Africa* (Westport, Conn.: Lawrence Hill & Co., 1976), p. 36-40.

14. *Ibid.*, p. 87.

15. International Monetary Fund, *International Financial Statistics,* January 1978.

16. U.S. Department of Commerce, *Overseas Business Reports,* "Market Profiles for Africa" (Washington, D.C.: Government Printing Office), December 1976.

17. U.S. Department of Commerce, *Overseas Business Reports,* "Sub-Saharan Africa: Further Growth Seen for U.S. Sales" (Washington, D.C.: Government Printing Office), November 1975, p. 2.

18. Summary of the report on "The Future of the World Economy," issued by the U.N. Department of Economic and Social

Affairs, as reported by The *New York Times,* October 14, 1976, p. 14; Lincoln Gordon, "Limits to the Growth Debate," *Resources,* no. 52, Summer 1976 (Resources for the Future); and U.S. Council on International Economic Policy, *Special Report: Critical Imported Materials* (Washington, D.C.: Government Printing Office), December, 1974, p. 13.

19. *Special Report: Critical Imported Materials,* p. 4.

20. *Ibid.,* p. 16.

21. "Major" is defined here as supplying more than 10% of the imports of a particular commodity.

22. Data on total world reserves were drawn from *Special Report: Critical Imported Materials, op. cit.* Data on the distribution of world reserves were taken from U.S. Bureau of Mines, U.S. Geological Survey, *Professional Paper 820.*

23. Congressional Budget Office, *U.S. Raw Materials Policy: Problems and Possible Solutions,* (Washington, D.C.: Government Printing Office), December 1976, p. 5.

24. *Special Report: Critical Imported Materials, op. cit.,* p. A-10.

25. In fact, in March of 1978 Citibank announced that it would no longer make loans to the government of South Africa.

26. Walter F. Hahn and Alvin J. Cottrell, *Soviet Shadow over Africa,* (Washington, D.C.: University of Miami, Center for Advanced International Studies, 1976), p. 105.

27. *Ibid,* p. 40.

Africa and the International Economy: A U.S. Response

Guy F. Erb

Since America's encounters with slave traders and, later, the privateers of the Barbary Coast, widespread misperceptions of Africa have been the backdrop for an American focus on individual crisis points. The Congo in the early 1960s, the Sahel in 1973-74, southern Africa at present are examples of crises that have not offset the ignorance of Africa which stems from the slight U.S. economic and political contacts with the continent.

Yet the limited U.S. political and economic interest in Africa seems certain to change for a variety of reasons. As other essays in this book emphasize, the situation in southern Africa will be a major and persistent issue for U.S. policy-makers in the years ahead. The transition to majority rule and political and economic developments in Zimbabwe/Rhodesia,

Namibia, and South Africa will be of increasing importance to the United States. Moreover, the prospective economic growth and development of Africa as a whole offers the United States an opportunity to so structure its trade and development assistance policies that they lay the foundations for a long-run interdependent relationship with African countries. In particular, the diversity of African resources provides an incentive to official and private American institutions to encourage new raw materials projects as well as to ensure a climate favorable to continued investment.

The present political ties between Africa and the United States, however, are relatively slight when compared to those of European countries. U.S. trade, aid, and investment links with the continent are also generally of less importance than those of the former colonial powers. The prospects for increasing U.S. economic relations with African nations and participation in raw materials development must be assessed in the light of the characteristics of the African economy and the approaches taken by the countries of the region to their domestic development as well as to international economic issues. Before turning to a review of U.S. economic policies toward Africa, this essay will therefore look briefly at the African economy and the economic relations of African states with the world economy and, in particular, at the points of contact between African trade and development priorities and the North-South negotiations between industrialized and developing countries.

Some Features of the African Economy

The characteristics of the African economy have been well summarized by Andrew Kamarck:

[61]

The continent is one of the two poorest regions in the world and it is still largely homogeneous in its poverty and in its economic structure, which consists of a fairly small modern sector and a large agricultural sector that absorbs most of the labor force. The modern sectors in most countries remain dependent on the export of a few primary products, with economic and financial relations with Western Europe still dominant. As in other developing regions, the rapid pace of urbanization, of growth in urban unemployment, and of overall population increase are becoming major problems.[1]

There are, of course, considerable differences within Africa: the countries of North Africa are moving toward integration with a Mediterranean economy, while different rates of economic growth in sub-Saharan Africa are contributing to the emergence of considerable gaps between the average incomes of the poorest and the relatively more advanced countries. When African nations are compared with other developing areas, however, the relative poverty of the continent stands out. Twenty-eight of the forty-five countries that were most seriously affected by the food and fuel price rises of recent years are in Africa, and eighteen of the twenty-nine internationally recognized "least-developed" countries are African states.[2] In 1974, only ten African countries had annual per capita incomes of more than $500.[3]

Trade

Africa's principal trading partners are in Western Europe, although Europe's share of African exports declined between 1965 and 1971 from 68 to 64 percent. Japan has made inroads in the minerals sector, and the United States is now a major importer of Nigerian petroleum. Only small quantities of manufactured goods are exported from African developing countries; therefore their main trade interests, despite efforts to diversify their resource-based economy, will remain in the primary products sector for several years to come.

Africa's trade with the rest of the world is characterized by reliance on the export of a relatively small number of raw materials. While a larger number of countries may be producers of a given primary product, a few nations often account for the bulk of export volume. For example, six African countries export copper, but most of Africa's share of world copper exports came from Zaire and Zambia, which between 1973 and 1974 exported 10 and 16 percent, respectively.[4] Similarly, 27 African countries export cotton, but Egypt was much the largest exporter, with 13 percent of world exports over the same time period. Sixteen African countries export cocoa, but Ghana, the Ivory Coast, and Nigeria between 1973 and 1974 exported more than 60 percent of the world's supply of cocoa. Primary commodity trade also tends to be concentrated in a small number of private firms in the developed world. For example, the leading company in the cocoa bean trade accounts for 20-30 percent of world trade.[5] The concentration of trade by country, commodity, and enterprise is associated with a high degree of instability in the export earnings of African countries, as recent price fluctuations of cocoa, coffee, sugar, and copper attest.

External Financial Resources

Direct private investment in Africa has been concentrated in the raw materials sector, particularly in the petroleum and mining industries. Most of the private investment has come from European countries. Indeed, U.S. investment outside South Africa, which has been a major recipient of private capital, remains at some 2 percent of total U.S. foreign investment. As Gordon Bertolin points out, this figure represents a decline since 1970, as a consequence of nationalizations.[6] The possibility of nationalization, expropriation, or forms of contractual agreements that increase the host country's share of a project's returns, tends to deter foreign investors in Africa. The ability of African and other developing countries to insist on contractual arrangements which go far beyond the traditional raw materials concessions has contributed to a certain reluctance on the part of companies to undertake large investments in the Third World.[7]

Much of Africa's mineral wealth is untapped. African countries hold 8 percent of the world's petroleum reserves, 90 percent of the world's cobalt, 40 percent of its platinum, 12 percent of its natural gas, and 30 percent of its uranium reserves, not to mention gold, copper, diamonds, cocoa, and bauxite. Moreover, much of the continent is still unsurveyed for raw materials, raising the prospect that substantial future discoveries may be made. Nevertheless, the immediate outlook for investment in many African countries is clouded, not only because of political uncertainties in southern Africa, but also because of unwillingness of many companies to face the risk of contract renegotiations or to accept what they regard as excessive demands by host countries in connection with new raw materials projects. U.S. investment flows are likely to increase only gradually, although there are indications that both companies and host countries are willing to consider the compromises that are necessary to mutually acceptable agreements.

Because of the relative underdevelopment of most African countries, they do not have much access to private capital markets. Only a few African countries have successfully drawn on Eurocurrency and other markets; those that have—Zaïre, for example—found that the commercial terms of such borrowings can be an onerous burden in times of depressed earnings from commodity exports.

Development assistance from developed countries and multilateral agencies has been of considerable importance to most African states, particularly the poorest among them, which have had little success in attracting significant private investments outside the minerals sector. Total African receipts of concessional aid from Western developed countries and multilateral agencies was $3.9 billion in 1975, 43 percent of the total net public and private flows of resources from these sources. U.S. bilateral aid flows have declined, from 11 percent of total U.S. bilateral aid in 1963, to some 7 percent in 1976. In current dollar terms, the 1976 level at $303 million is about two-thirds the 1963 high. In 1974, U.S. net official development assistance was only about one-fifth the aid flow of some $2.3 billion from European members of the Development Assistance Committee.[8] According to estimates for 1975, assistance to Africa from the Soviet Union is declining while that of the People's Republic of China has increased, although total flows from both these sources remain far below those from Western donor countries. (Estimates for 1975 place total Russian disbursements to all developing countries at $350 million and total Chinese disbursements at $375 million.)[9] Disbursements from members of the Organization of Petroleum Exporting Countries (OPEC) and the multilateral agencies they have established have risen rapidly, and OPEC commitments remain at high levels. In 1975 OPEC commitments to all African countries were $4.1 billion, while OPEC commitments to African countries *not* members of the Arab League were nearly $400 million in that year. Disbursements

[65]

TABLE 1

African Food production Trends
Average Annual Increase

(Percentages)

	1962-73	1970-75
Africa	2.7	0.7
All developing countries	2.7	2.1
World	2.7	2.0

Source: World Food Council, Increasing Food Production in Developing Countries, WFC/20, 1976, cited in M. J. Williams, Chairman, Development Assistance Committee, *Development Cooperation, 1976 Review* (Paris: OECD, November 1976), p. 133.

from the Special Arab Fund for Africa rose from $24 million in 1974 to $118 million in 1975.[10]

Food

In the 1970s attention focused on the food crisis of the Sahelian countries. The effects of the prolonged drought that those countries experienced were mitigated only after considerable international intervention. The situation in the Sahel is certainly difficult, but Africa as a whole is a food-deficit region and recent rates of growth of total food production are far from satisfactory. Climatological and soil conditions, insufficient inputs of capital and technology, and inadequate means of providing credit to farmers all play a role in depressing rates of food production.

[66]

The decline in food production rates during 1970-75 is particularly worrisome, given population and urbanization trends. A study by the International Food Policy Research Institute projects annual grain deficits for sub-Saharan Africa of between 13.7 and 14.9 million tons by 1985-86. Low income countries, those with per capita incomes of under $200, account for between 4.1 and 4.8 million tons of that estimate. Within the group of "high" income African nations, Nigeria is seen as facing particularly large grain deficits by the mid-1980s. A continuation of large regional food deficits is likely unless additional national and international measures are taken. Thus domestic policies and external assistance which aim at increasing food production and their relationship to the use of food aid will be of great importance in Africa in coming years.

AFRICA IN THE GLOBAL ECONOMY

Despite the undoubted points of contact between Marxist-Leninist ideology and African concerns over the continent's external economic and political dependence, Western countries in general, and particularly those of Europe, exert the strongest pull on the political, economic, and commercial development of African nations. Moreover, African and other developing countries address nearly all their calls for international economic reform to the Western industrialized nations.

Africa and a New International Economic Order

In 1974, African countries, together with other members of the "Group of 77" (which now includes over 120 countries),

[67]

brought together the major international economic issues which had been debated in the 1960s in a U.N. resolution calling for the establishment of a New International Economic Order (NIEO). The claims now made in the North-South negotiations cap a decade of largely fruitless efforts by the developing countries to gain a hearing for their international economic proposals.

Essentially an attempt to alter the structures through which influence is wielded in the international economy, the NIEO declaration called for measures concerning raw materials and primary commodities, food, transportation and insurance, international monetary reform, industrialization, the transfer of technology and transnational corporations, and greater cooperation among developing countries.[11] Eastern European countries, whose relatively small involvement in the world economy would limit their participation in NIEO debates in any event, also claim that they bear no responsibility for the underdevelopment of the Third World. They have thus tried to remain on the margin of confrontations between the industrialized countries and the Third World, a policy that has subjected them to increasing criticism from developing nations. China, in contrast, has actively championed the Third World cause while avoiding categorization as a developed nation.

The Western countries were thus the main targets of the NIEO demands. Following the confrontation of 1974, attempts in 1975, 1976 and 1977 to reconcile the opposing positions yielded only slight results. NIEO demands remain on the table: A recent African statement on global cooperation—considered by the *Club de Dakar*—included proposals for the (1) transfer of resources from industrialized and OPEC countries, (2) preferential development of industries in the Third World, (3) stabilization of export earnings, (4) management of nonrenewable resources, and (5) application of research findings to development problems.

During the North-South debates the overall African position has shifted from confrontation over the principles of reform to an insistence on measures that would serve the region's immediate interests. In 1974, the tone of U.N. and other debates was confrontational: Algeria staked out a strong "radical" leadership position in the Third World, and African support for OPEC and the Algerian position was high. On both political and economic issues African nations lined up against the industrialized world as the developing countries launched their proposals for a New International Economic Order. However, during 1975, OPEC aid transfers to non-Arab countries failed to live up to expectations, and Algeria's leadership came under pressure from the "moderates" in the Third World. African support for a confrontational approach to NIEO issues appeared to decline with the successful conclusion of the negotiations with the European Community over the Lomé Convention, and the emergence of Nigeria and other sub-Saharan African countries to positions of leadership within the developing countries. In their approach to negotiations with developed countries, African states were supported by both the U.N. Economic Commission for Africa and the Organization of African Unity.

African countries have great needs for external financial resources, and they depend on unstable earnings from a few primary commodities for the bulk of their external receipts. The Lomé negotiations illustrated the consequent willingness of African nations to seek immediate benefits, such as aid transfers or tariff preferences, in their bargaining with industrialized countries where there was a reasonable prospect of success. Achievement of such measures, however limited in impact they might be, has made African countries reluctant to embrace broad multilateral proposals of uncertain effect and problematical implementation. When international measures are at stake, the group of African nations has usually emphasized the resource transfers that can be obtained by them. For example, during the 1977 negotiations within the United Nations Conference on Trade and Development (UNCTAD) on primary commodity price stabilization, and in particular on a common fund for buffer stocks, the African group insisted on a version of the fund which would have combined price stabilization with "other measures" to increase production, processing, and diversification. By emphasizing such "aid" functions for the common fund, the African group placed its members' interests in expanded resource transfers above the possible impact of that position on (1) relations with other developing countries that could agree to a more modest fund, and (2) the prospects for a negotiated agreement with developed countries and oil exporters, neither of which favored the expansion of the common fund's activities into long-term finance. Apparently convinced that price stabilization alone offered little to Africa, the group of African countries clung tenaciously to their view of the common fund, a tactic that began to resemble their confrontational approach of 1974. In this instance, however, not only were institutional relations between rich and poor nations at stake, but also the amounts of resources reaching African economies.

AFRICA AND EUROPE: THE LOMÉ CONVENTION

While African nations have generally backed the calls of the Third World for major changes in the international economy, their dealings with the industrialized countries of Europe differ from those of other developing countries. A number of

African countries have successfully negotiated concessions with European nations, first in the Yaoundé agreements with the six-member European Economic Community (EEC), and then in the Lomé Convention with the nine members of the expanded community. African nations have tended to be pragmatic in their approach to negotiations with the EEC. In these negotiations, African states have shown a willingness to compromise in order to obtain their objectives and have generally maintained a unified position both toward Europe and other developing countries.

In the mid-1960s, the division between the countries participating in the Yaoundé agreements and Latin American nations was one of the most significant fissures in the façade of Third World solidarity. At the 1967 Algiers Conference of the Group of 77 developing countries, for example, only long negotiations and a last-minute compromise organized by the UNCTAD Secretary-General, Raul Prebisch, brought the Latin American and African countries to a joint position on the question of generalized tariff preferences. Comparable divisions between Africa and Latin America have also emerged in the 1970s over commodity policies and the common fund for buffer stocks. Asian developing countries have usually been content to associate themselves with whatever compromises emerge from the Latin American-African confrontation.

The negotiations concluded in 1975 between the European Community and forty-six African, Caribbean, and Pacific (ACP) countries that established the Lomé Convention were different from other North-South negotiations. The Convention has been described as the first step toward a New International Economic Order. However, its relevance to the evolution of new economic systems lies primarily in the fact that it was *jointly* negotiated between developed and developing countries. In the Lome talks, a unified group of developing countries sought and obtained uniform policy measures from a group of industrialized nations. In contrast, developed countries now implement the UNCTAD-sponsored systems of tariff preferences with a wide variety of national schemes that contain many different sorts of restrictions on preferential tariff treatment. Moreover, until the conclusion of the negotiations on the International Fund for Agricultural Development in 1976, negotiations on international financial mechanisms, such as the International Development Association, had been primarily among donor countries; the developing nations occupied a secondary position while "burden sharing" issues were hammered out within the developed-country group.

Although the Convention is far from being a perfect instrument of North-South cooperation, it does contain measures of considerable interest to the participating developing countries, which now number fifty-two. In addition to the roughly $4 billion to be transferred through EEC financial institutions during the 1976-80 period, the Lomé Convention covers trade cooperation, stabilization of export earnings (through the STABEX scheme), and provisions relating to the treatment of companies and firms as well as payments and capital movements. There are also institutional measures establishing on-going mechanisms for consultation and cooperation between the Community and the associated ACP countries.

The Lomé Convention provides preferential treatment for the exports of ACP countries, but the majority of signatories, particularly those in Africa, are so heavily dependent on commodity trade that tariff preferences for manufactured goods do not provide short-run gains comparable to those which could be obtained from commodity policy initiatives. Nevertheless, African countries do have a long-run interest in exports of manufactured products, and the provisions for industrial cooperation in the Lomé Convention, while of limited short-run benefit to most ACP nations, offer potential gains to their relatively underdeveloped industrial sectors.

The importance that African countries attach to the Lomé Convention derives from the role that European nations have played in the modernization of the region and the influence which the former colonial powers still exert in many countries. The measures embodied in the Convention, the strong presence of European official and private sectors in a number of African countries, and the area's strong dependence on European trade and investment add up to a formidable component of the African political-economic scene. The Convention is, moreover, an example of what can be achieved jointly by African and other developing states.

The United States, separated from the continent by history and with links to individual countries that are small relative to Europe's, can do little at present to match or "compete" directly with the Euro-African cooperation of the Lomé Convention. The United States can, however, adopt bilateral and multilateral policies which respond to African interests. Such policies, part of a globally oriented approach to economic issues, might well compare favorably to the actions of other developed nations and illustrate the seriousness of the U.S. intent to foster African economic development. For example, the global alternative to the STABEX mechanism of the Lomé Convention is the compensatory financing facility of the International Monetary Fund. Although the STABEX is frequently cited as a model for other international arrangements to stabilize export earnings, it is capable of providing far fewer resources to African states than is the IMF facility. STABEX does contain several positive elements—two are its grants to the poorest countries and interest-free loans to the other participants in the scheme. But the IMF facility could be modified to incorporate improvements which would draw upon the STABEX example while maintaining the IMF scheme's advantages, notably the substantially greater resources that it can provide. Improvement of the IMF facility would probably not dissuade African states from seeking further concessions from the EEC as they renegotiate the Lomé Convention in 1980. However, U.S. support for the enhancement of an important source of multilateral finance for African nations would demonstrate the relevance to them of international policies that are not tied to a particular group of industrialized countries.

U.S. Economic Policies Toward Africa

Participating in the economic and social development of African countries, contributing to an increase in the food production capacity, fostering a gradual increase in trade and investment ties with the region, and improving the prospects for mutually acceptable agreements on natural resource development are all valid objectives for U.S. economic policies. But the connections between American economic policies toward Africa and U.S. political and security objectives in the area should also be explored. Let us assume that (1) the United States will support as peaceful a transition as possible to majority rule in southern Africa, and (2) the United States will stop short of military assistance to liberation movements in southern Africa, and (3) that its political initiatives or responses to African demands will, on more than one occasion, fail to satisfy the leaders of the front-line countries or the liberation movements in Zimbabwe, Namibia, and South Africa.

[74]

Since the United States cannot expect to persuade African states to accept all aspects of the U.S. approach to southern Africa, U.S. political objectives could be served by American support for economic policies which could significantly assist African development. By demonstrating a U.S. commitment to Africa, constructive economic policies could smooth the U.S. involvement in the difficult transition to majority rule in southern Africa as well as provide an incentive to African countries to respond constructively to other U.S. policy initiatives. A U.S. economic policy response to Africa could not, of course, ensure the acceptance by African states of American proposals. An approach which coordinated economic policies with U.S. political objectives could not, for example, offset negative African reactions to what they saw as a seriously deficient policy regarding majority rule (nor would adequate political measures absolve U.S. policy makers from addressing the trade, investment, and resource issues that are at the center of U.S. economic concerns).

American economic policies that met some of the basic concerns of African states could, however, gain for the United States a hearing as a credible and responsible participant in the long-run development of the region. As a major power and deeply involved participant in the talks aimed at resolving southern African issues, the United States, acting in the political arena alone, would have an impact on the course of events in the area. However, in an atmosphere of increasing African militancy toward southern Africa, a failure to buttress political initiatives with economic policies that address the problems of the region as a whole risks a decline in influence over the attitudes of African countries and their actions toward the minority-ruled areas.

If American economic policies toward Africa are to demonstrate a seriousness of purpose regarding African development,

[75]

they must go beyond the commonly heard rhetorical support for international cooperation. The U.S. commitment would have to be wide in geographic scope and content. Interaction with nations other than those that are closest to southern Africa would be a necessary contribution to a broadly based African response to U.S. initiatives. Development assistance through bilateral and multilateral channels, including the African Development Fund, trade policies for both manufactured goods and commodities, and private investment would all be important parts of an adequate U.S. economic policy package toward Africa.

Development Assistance and Debt Management

African countries have negotiated considerable development assistance transfers from Europe. U.S. bilateral assistance in Africa and U.S. support for an expansion of multilateral lending in the region, in particular, from the International Development Association and the African Development Fund will be critical elements of U.S. economic policies toward the region. Increases in U.S. financial transfers will be the starting point of official attempts to widen economic ties between the United States and Africa. Progress toward development cooperation with some African countries will be complicated, however, by two aspects of current U.S. policy: its attention to human rights issues and to meeting the basic human needs of the peoples in recipient countries.

The human rights issue is drawn most sharply with respect to South Africa and Uganda. In other more ambiguous cases, however, human rights criteria may also diminish aid to individual countries. Human rights criteria may also be used to cut off aid to leftist regimes like that in Mozambique. In such cases, their application may prove a significant obstacle to U.S. political objectives. Generally, however, this should not affect the overall direction and magnitude of the U.S. bilateral assistance program.

The basic human needs approach to development assistance, if administered in a way that stresses the development of peoples' abilities to feed, clothe, and house themselves, will pose no long-run obstacle to effective cooperation between donors and recipient countries. At present, both are exploring the implications which the basic human needs approach has for development policy and individual projects. After a transition period, which may be marked by a reluctance on the part of African and other developing countries to accept what they may see as another "intervention" from the developed world, the basic human needs strategy will almost certainly be incorporated into a wide variety of national and international measures for economic and social development.

Because trade liberalization and commodity measures face opposition from important sectors of U.S. labor and industry, an expansion of the bilateral aid program to Africa might appear to be an "easy" policy to adopt in support of U.S. political objectives. However, an approach which based U.S. economic policies toward Africa primarily on aid flows would face some major problems. First, as welcome as it would be, U.S. development assistance would be evaluated relative to European and OPEC flows to the region, both of which are substantial. Second, to have an impact on African attitudes toward U.S. policies the assistance would need to have a broad geographic scope; programs aimed principally at southern Africa would not meet this criterion. Third, if past experience is to be a guide, proposals for expanded U.S. aid programs will meet opposition within the executive branch and Congress; if congressional opposition, for example, prevented the implementation of announced programs, the consequent African disappointment would certainly be harmful to the attainment of U.S. policy objectives. Finally, since aid is a notoriously uncertain means of gaining "friends" in foreign nations, and because grants or loans cannot meet all the development objectives of recipient countries, U.S. development assistance should be an important part, but not the sole component, of economic policies in the region.

The overall debt problem of the developing world has been the focus of increasing concern by both donor and recipient nations. The developing nations themselves have made several proposals, of which the following are the most relevant to African nations: (1) cancellation of the bilateral debt of the least developed, land-locked, and island nations; (2) a repayment moratorium, at the very least, for the countries most seriously affected by the oil price action; and (3) additional program assistance from multilateral financial institutions to developing country debtors in amounts which would at least match the service on debt owed to these same institutions.

Currently, most African external debt is owed to official, not private, institutions, since the access of most countries to private lending has been limited. In 1974 total African official and officially guaranteed debt was over $28 billion, according to the World Bank. By the end of 1976, the total may have reached $35 billion or $40 billion. Big borrowers include Egypt with $7.3 billion outstanding by the end of 1976, Zaire with $1.9 billion, Zambia with $1.2 billion, and Tanzania with just under $1.0 billion.[12]

The debt of African nations (in absolute terms or relative to their "debt service capacity") may not appear sufficient to justify a moratorium or even a rescheduling of payments. However, debt relief, while subject to serious complications, could assist the development of the poorest countries and reach

[78]

those most in need of assistance. In those cases where severe short-run debt problems emerge, the developed countries can be expected to support rescheduling of debt and longer-run measures intended to strengthen the economies of debtor countries. Moreover, attention to the direction of development lending is required to ensure that it does contribute to the long-run ability of African nations to reduce their dependence on external resources; food production and the generation of export capacity should receive a high priority in U.S. aid programs.

Trade and Investment Policies

There are three main issues on which the United States and African countries can seek mutually beneficial trade and investment policies: (1) liberalization of barriers to trade, (2) the stabilization of commodity prices and the export earnings of primary produce exporters, and (3) the development of the raw materials of the region.

The United States is currently seeking the liberalization of trade barriers with both developed and developing countries in the multilateral trade negotiations among members and non-members of the General Agreement on Tariffs and Trade (GATT). Thus far, developed-country measures to increase the manufactured exports of the Third World—through preferential tariffs or multilateral trade liberalization—have not led to very significant benefits for African countries. One important factor is the current composition of African exports. Manufactured goods are the main focus of the negotiations, and the more advanced developing nations, most of which are outside of Africa, have had the most success in this area. Zaire and Zambia had exports of manufactures of more than $500 million in 1973, but nonferrous metals accounted for nearly all their manufactured exports. When petroleum products and nonferrous metals are excluded, only Algeria, Morocco, Ghana, and the Ivory Coast had exports of manufactures in excess of $100 million in 1973.[13]

Through special measures for developing nations in the trade negotiations and preferential tariff treatment for their exports, the United States is committed to improving the trade prospects of African and other developing countries. But although the U.S. tariff preference system is intended to shift trade toward the poorer developing countries, its impact on their trade has been limited. Measures are needed to make the trade system as a whole, and preferential systems in particular, more responsive to the needs of African and other relatively less developed countries. Liberalization of barriers facing tropical products and manufactured goods within the multilateral trade negotiations and allowances for developing nations in trade policy codes on nontariff measures are possible means of providing greater benefits from trade to developing countries.

With regard to commodity policy, an area of great immediate concern to African states, the United States is committed to negotiate with primary product exporters on individual commodity agreements and a common fund for buffer stocks. Although many in developed countries favor compensatory finance to stabilize *earnings* from commodity exports, rather than commodity prices, the developing nations have insisted on the price measures which were drawn together by the UNCTAD Secretariat in its integrated commodity program.[14] The compensatory finance provided by STABEX and the IMF facility to stabilize earnings is useful to raw materials exporters, but the two mechanisms cannot be expected to reduce the efforts of developing countries to obtain more control over raw materials production in their countries and over the operations of world commodity markets. To illustrate, in 1976, a year of heavy drawings on the IMF facility and of the first transfers from STABEX, developing-country interests in the UNCTAD's integrated commodity program were at their highest. The UNCTAD proposals for an integrated approach to commodity policy include suggestions for commodity agreements, a common fund for buffer stock financing, improved compensatory financing, mutual commitments by importers and exporters, and greater processing of raw materials in developing countries. Ten "core" commodities have been chosen for special attention, and the African trade interest in many of them is significant.

Having committed themselves to negotiations on agreements to govern trade in some commodities and to consultations on others regarding the feasibility of price stabilization accords, the United States and other raw-materials-consuming countries must now decide whether their interests would be served best by their participation in, or absence from, the management of commodity agreements and a common fund. The United States is negotiating actively with African and other developing countries on the UNCTAD commodity proposals; agreements in particular commodities among producer and consumer countries are emerging slowly, and the negotiations on a common fund remain far short of conclusion.[15]

Another U.S. approach, attempted without success in 1976, would be to propose alternatives to the UNCTAD program. One such proposal was an international resources bank, whose investment guarantees were intended to encourage the flow of investment to raw materials projects in developing countries. That mechanism would have addressed a serious problem

[81]

stemming from the confrontation between companies and host countries over the forms of contractual agreements. But this proposal related to commodity *production* and did not meet the concerns of the Group of 77 over commodity *market* issues, namely, price and earnings fluctuations. The investment guarantees of the resources bank could have been a complement to commodity policy initiatives, but as this was interpreted as an attempt to divert attention from commodity agreements and the common fund, it was rejected.

Thus there appears to be little prospect that international insurance schemes or formalized intermediary functions for multilateral financial institutions will be created to foster new materials development. There are, however, a number of ways in which that objective can be achieved. National systems of investment insurance, for example, can play a role in raw materials projects. Or, the problems between host countries and private investors might be ameliorated by an expansion of the participation of multilateral institutions in raw materials financing. The World Bank has already decided to expand its lending for minerals and energy. Regional banks are expected to do so as well. The finance available from international financial institutions is limited, and their role as intermediaries will be constrained by the number and kind of conditions host countries and private entities are willing to accept. The World Bank Group and regional development banks are, however, in a position to help satisfy private investors' concerns, and help the host governments gain more influence over raw materials development. Multilateral institutions could also help bring together private institutions to finance raw materials projects and facilitate access by developing-country governments or state enterprises to capital markets in industrialized areas. Increased multilateral finance would thus complement the

[82]

consuming countries' interest in adequate and reasonably priced supplies of raw materials and the private sector's desire to reduce investment risks in the raw materials sector.

If coupled with programs to foster the processing of raw materials and the diversification of production in primary-product-exporting countries, such multilateral investment policies could meet the objectives of the African nations that now seek to introduce long-run finance functions into the operation of the common fund. If developed and developing countries are able to agree on the timing and size of the common fund's operations—and on the assignment of raw materials financing to the international financial institutions—they would have achieved a compromise from which producing and consuming countries could gain. One cannot imagine that multilateral financial institutions can resolve all disputes among investors and host countries, nor that commodity agreements supported by a common fund would dampen all price fluctuations. But increased lending from international development banks to the raw materials sector plus the stabilization operations of a common fund should be able to contribute to the stability of both investment flows and commodity prices, with consequent benefits for Africa and the world economy as a whole.

A U.S. policy to improve economic relations with African states and at the same time complement American political initiatives in southern Africa would include a variety of measures for trade and development assistance. Special attention to African priorities within the framework of multilateral negotiations and a sharper focus on Africa in American bilateral policies would be required in a credible response to the trade and aid claims of African states. It is unlikely that either U.S. or African interests will be entirely satisfied by policies such as those described above. But the pragmatism that has characterized African approaches to international economic issues makes it likely that African states will seriously consider U.S. economic initiatives in the context of their domestic development programs and their goals for the political evolution of the continent as a whole.

NOTES

1. Andrew M. Kamarck, "Sub-Saharan Africa in the 1980s: An Economic Profile," in Helen Kitchen, ed., *Africa: From Mystery to Maze* (Lexington: Lexington Books, 1976), p. 167.

2. Maurice J. Williams, Chairman, Development Assistance Committee, *Development Co-operation, 1976 Review* (Paris: Organisation for Economic Co-operation and Development, November 1976), pp. 197-98.

3. Algeria, Angola, Gabon, Libya, Mauritius, Reunion, Rhodesia (Zimbabwe), South Africa, Tunisia, and Zambia. See Table A-3, Statistical Annexes, in John W. Sewell, and the Staff of the Overseas Development Council, *The United States and World Development: Agenda 1977* (New York: Praeger Publishers, Inc.), for the Overseas Development Council, 1977).

4. *Ibid.*, pp. 198-99.

5. G. K. Helleiner, "Freedom and Management in International Commodity Markets: U.S. Imports from Developing Countries," *World Development,* Vol. 6, No. 1 (1978).

6. Cf. Chapter 2, above.

7. See Guy F. Erb, "Issues Affecting Trade and Investment in

Non-Fuel Minerals," *Case Western Reserve Journal of International Law,* Vol. 8, No. 2 (Spring 1976).

8.   William I. Jones, "The Search for an Aid Policy," in Kitchen, ed., *Africa: from Mystery to Maze,* p. 357; this figure includes all contributions to multilateral agencies except for IBRD, IFC, and ADF. See also, U.S. AID, *U.S. Overseas Loans and Grants* (Washington, D.C., 1971 and 1975), pp. 82 and 85, respectively.

9.   Williams, op. cit., p. 63.

10.   Williams, op. cit., Chapter V, Tables V-6, V-12, V-18, and V-19.

11.   Guy F. Erb, "North-South Negotiations and Compensatory Financing," Overseas Development Council, June 8, 1977.

12.   Harold Van B. Cleveland and W. H. Bruce Brittain, "Are the LDC's in Over Their Heads," *Foreign Affairs,* July 1977, p. 734.

13.   *UNCTAD, Trade in Manufactures of Developing Countries and Territories, 1974 Review* (New York: United Nations Document E.76.II.D.8, 1976), pp. 26-29 and 51-60.

14.   For an analysis of the integrated program and U.S. policies, see Guy F. Erb and Bart S. Fisher, "U.S. Commodity Policy: What Response to Third World Initiatives?", in *Law and Policy in International Business,* Vol. 9, No. 2, pp. 479-514.

15.   Editor's note: African states participating in the UNCTAD negotiations for a common fund strongly favor an expansion of the fund's activities to include measures other than price stabilization. African support for a "second window" of a common fund that could support diversification of commodity production and marketing

activities, for example, was a factor contributing to the suspension, in November 1977, of an UNCTAD negotiation on the common fund. The developed countries were divided on this issue, and the Group of 77 as a whole supported the African position. The differences between the two groups proved irreconcilable at the UNCTAD meeting.

[THREE]

Coming Political Problems
In Black Africa

I. William Zartman

Now that Africa has recovered political control over its destiny from colonial rulers, it is struggling with the more complex, subtle, and elusive problem of giving content to that formal independence. The continent covered by the generalization "Africa" contains a large variety of poorly developed countries with vulnerable economies, unintegrated societies, and unstable polities that are jealous of their fragile independence and frequently have difficulty in getting along with each other. America's interactions with these states in coming years and its policies toward them will be triggered primarily by problems arising within the African states. This chapter addresses itself to coming political problems in black Africa, and to some possible responses. The focus is on the short and middle range, mainly covering the remaining years of the decade and, at most, stretching into the early years of the 1980s.

On the policy side, there is a "point of view." But it is neither that of Santa Claus nor that of a sheriff, two figures who seem to have dominated the debate on Africa to date. To be sure, foreign policy should leave the world better once it has been effected, and it does have to meet challenges from current opponents. But more than that, it should above all seek to defend the interests of the policy-making state interpreted within the context of the common interests of all, and it should show initiative and innovation in a positive attempt to help solve problems.

But is the United States actually "interested" in Africa, and should it be? What are the bases of these interests? The questions are especially pertinent in regard to a continent where American interests in the usual sense—trade, investment, bases, traditional responsibilities, historic involvements—are admittedly lower than elsewhere. In a post-interventionist world, the most appealing argument would be one for noninvolvement, if it could be made. Even in terms of détente, if Africa is so problem-laden, why not just leave it alone, in the knowledge that even if the Russians or Chinese took it on, they would never be able to handle it?

The starting point of such a reasoning process lies in a proper appreciation of Africa in the cold war or détente, or America's position toward Russia and China vis-à-vis Africa, but the conclusion of the argument must lie in an awareness of American interests toward Africa itself. Communist strategy for development includes mobilization of political and economic energies within a centrally planned and controlled system, along with mobilization of discontent against an external—necessarily Western—scapegoat. The mobilization of energies is a positive approach to development when it works, but there are as yet no examples of success in Africa, and few at all outside of the fully mobilized Communist societies of Asia and Cuba. The centralized system of planning and control is a major weakness at the crucial core of the system, since planners have generally lacked the omniscience necessary for their job and control suppresses the pluralism that is so important as a corrective. The focusing of discontent on Western scapegoats is the most unpalatable aspect of Communist control from the American point of view, for it provides a permanent bias against cooperation with the West on common concerns. Finally, East-leaning regimes have a tendency to spread their good news throughout the neighborhood. In Africa, with the likely return of ideological politics, the rise of distributional issues, and the generation of new counter-elites in the 1980s, the coming decade will find the continent as vulnerable to subversion and opposition movements in exile as it was in the early 1960s, and governments of true believers willing to give aid and sanctuary to such activities will be deeply destabilizing.

There is no reason to adopt a different attitude toward Communist powers' attempts to win over African countries than has been adopted toward such efforts elsewhere in the world. It is in America's interest that Russian and Chinese influence be as limited as possible; there does not seem to be any reason to imagine that the United States can safely engage in joint ventures and joint responses to African problems with the Soviet Union, as we might do from time to time—in the Sahel, for example—with other Western nations.

In the context of the global balance and beyond it, America's interest in Africa is primarily political: It lies in a need to monitor the continent's chaotic development in order to help avoid destabilizing crises which would subvert African progress and suck the United States into unwanted but unavoidable intervention. The United States has an interest in a stable African development process in order to prevent the many potential instances of instability and conflict from overcoming the frail possibilities of progress and resulting in wider conflict and crisis. However, it should be emphasized that the United States has no direct responsibilities in Africa and, on the other side of the coin, cannot count on African states as allies. African states are continually seeking to borrow power on a short-term basis as local conflicts escalate, despite the continental injunction to seek African solutions for African problems; but such temporary loans respond very little to the interest of the outside power and more frequently signify an internationalization of a conflict whose extension beyond the continent is not justified by more lasting affinities.

The absence of direct responsibilities in Africa leaves American policy with great freedom of choice regarding the allocation of limited resources. The United States is therefore free to deal with African needs on their merits. It can also bring a greater reach of responses and initiatives to face the problems associated with underdevelopment and the conflicts growing out of the development process.

I. Resource Problems

Underdevelopment can be summarized, among other ways, as a penury of resources, human as well as material. Two resource problems stand out in underdeveloped Africa: one—the food supply—involving short supply, and the other—arms purchases—misplaced demand.

1. Africa is increasingly unable to feed itself. Its per capita food production has remained constant over the past twenty years and in the absence of serious changes cannot be expected to increase faster than population growth in the next decade. There are four ingredients to this situation. First, traditional

agriculture is increasingly incapable of feeding even the rural population, which is growing, though at a slower rate than the rest. Second, population growth is more rapid than the growth of modern agriculture, since the drain of the towns, the clogging of commercial circuits, and the sparsity of farm credits and facilities all work to remove incentives from the primary sector. Third, where agriculture is favored, it is oriented to export crops which earn hard currency for urban commercial, administrative, and industrial growth. Fourth, in some areas—notably but not only the Sahel—all these factors, aggravated by climatic effects, serve to undermine the defense of marginally arable land against the desert.

Potentially, sub-Saharan Africa is estimated to be cultivating only 27 percent of its 643 million hectares of "suitable agricultural land" and producing less than 1 percent of its maximum agricultural production of $11,681 \times 10^8$ kilograms of consumable protein. But actually, an estimated quarter-million hectares are lost to the Sahara in an average year, cereal deficits will triple in the poorer states by 1985 and may increase 25-fold in Nigeria, and agriculture for domestic consumption continues to lose ground to export production. Simple ecological defense is beyond the present means of most of the affected states, reclamation faster than population growth beyond the means of any of them, and an increase in productivity possible only through massive imports of capital and technology.

Food is a political problem. Governments must either make a major effort to change agricultural policies, depend on increasingly large food imports (either as purchased goods or as public aid), or face basic problems of insecurity or unrest. Complacent governments have fallen because of this in the past decade (e.g., Niger, Chad, Mali, Ethiopia) and others will fall in the 1980s. Food purchases, even when possible, deplete

[91]

scarce currency reserves; food aid poses serious political problems of intervention, reliance, and dependence. The first option—intensified agricultural production—is preferable as well as possible. But a policy of agricultural growth requires elements of control, mobilization, technology, and implementation—not to speak of resources—that African states have not shown to date.

Some of these elements could be provided through an American assistance program that would help develop agricultural extension services in those African countries that are willing and able to complement the aid with their own contributions. The program can provide seeds, fertilizers, training and technology, as direct inputs and as incentives to governments to make the necessary structural and attitudinal changes in agriculture. Its training component is particularly important. The impact of the program—and American leadership—would be magnified if it were channeled through the U.N's Food and Agricultural Organization (FAO) or, better yet, through its Economic Commission for Africa (ECA) or the Organization of African Unity (OAU) as the impetus for a larger international effort, or if it were combined with other Development Assistance Committee (DAC) donors into a multinational (Western) program. The goal of the program would be to develop basic agricultural self-sufficiency and regional export capability in those African states willing and able to utilize the assistance.

It should be obvious that the ability to feed itself is both the most basic capability of a society and the weakest link in the African economies. It is therefore an area where African needs are greatest, compounded by worsening cycles of political instability and underdevelopment if they are not met—and where America can make a coherent, coordinated contribution. if effective, such a program can mitigate the danger of the terrible droughts and endemic loss of land in the Sahel and similar regions, or at least can enable other African countries to provide agricultural aid when drought strikes the weaker regions. That is certainly a more effective use of scarce resources than the PL-480 program of direct food aid, which builds dependency rather than self-reliance, and resentment rather than gratitude in addition. Such a program could mobilize and exhibit some of America's most famous qualities—know-how, pragmatism, the use of science for humanity, the spirit of collective barn-raising, among others— to attack a basic problem whose solution is in both American and African interests.

2. The other great problem is that Africa is increasingly in danger of seeing its scarce resources going into arms races. Despite some high percentage increases in military expenditures with the initial establishment of armies after independence, Africa today is the least armed continent in the world and imports the fewest arms. Its countries have a low average of 1.9 soldiers per thousand civilians, and a somewhat higher average of 2.7 for those countries with military regimes. Its average per capita military expenditures of $6.70 in 1975 were also the world's lowest. Nonetheless, they are felt. The average African country's military expenditure was two-thirds of its expenditure for education and more than double (225 percent) its spending on health. In military regimes, the average per capita military expenditure rises only slightly, to $7, but social expenditures are lower, so that the average military regime's expenditure for defense is as high as its expenditure on education and almost three times as high as on health. Although these figures include personnel expenditures, the part that goes for arms is not only a budgetary drag but also a currency drain, since all arms are imported. Only South Africa and Rhodesia have their own armaments industry.

[93]

There are a half-dozen reasons why African states buy arms, none of them a good one in a continent where boundaries are legitimized by common agreement, where imperial recolonization and cold war satellization are not real possibilities, and where atomic arms are militarily inappropriate and still absent. The first and classical reason to arm is for general defense and deterrence. The second and third relate to the two open conflicts in which African states are directly concerned: the Palestine and the southern African disputes. Fourth, there are potential border conflicts to guard against. Fifth, paradoxically, arms races can serve as a symbolic surrogate for open military conflict. This effect (which has occurred in Latin America and even among the cold war protagonists) in Africa has involved Morocco and Algeria, Zaire and Congo, Kenya and Uganda, Ethiopia and Somalia, among others. Unfortunately, there is no guarantee that rivalry in arms purchases will eliminate the use of these same arms.

Finally, arms purchases can also be motivated by domestic conflicts and rivalries. In some cases, arms are needed for internal police actions, as in the civil wars which have troubled Sudan, Ethiopia, and Chad for over a decade. In others, they feed the rivalries among military branches, as in Ghana, Algeria, Uganda, and Ethiopia (in each contributing directly to a military coup).

It can be seen from this rapid enumeration that most of these motivations for arms purchases are self-stoking fires, causes so broadly applicable that they can lead to arms races in the most mechanical sense and can set up competition between any pair of neighbors. In addition, some of these actually lead to other, unintended, destabilizing effects, such as coups by one of several internally competing military factions or by the military forces of the loser (or even just non-winner) in a territorial dispute (as in Algeria, Sudan, Ethiopia, and Chad, among others). External uses of the military in Africa have generally been exercises in self-exhaustion, in which the outcome (usually return to the status quo) has been the result, not of one side's victory but of both sides' depletion of their first-string resources before ever arriving at a decisive battle. This general pattern was in the process of being upset in the Horn of Africa in 1977 and 1978, where some decisive confrontations occurred, a large piece of territory changed hands, and the parties went beyond their initial stocks into new arms supplies, before returning to the status quo, at least temporarily. The exception only gives further support for the judgment, however, that foreign arms supplies are a destabilizing, escalating venture.

There is another reason for arms sales: the effectiveness of the salesmen in search for markets, allies, and other advantages. In the early 1970s, France was the largest arms supplier for Africa, with Russia second, Britain third, the United States fourth, and the diversified fifth category of "other" selling more than the Soviet Union. Generally, a simple effect noted elsewhere in the world determines the quantity of purchases: the rank of African states among the arms purchasers in the continent is a function of their rank by total GNP. Among the larger states, Rhodesia, Ethiopia and Sudan have moved upward, out of order, in military expenditures, and Ivory Coast is a downward exception. A number of states are overarmed, with quantities and levels of armaments that they cannot absorb, use, or afford.

While such arms sales may be good for the supplier's arms industry, it is less certain that they are very effective in buying useful or reliable relations with the purchaser. In some cases, African states have practiced diversification as an antidote to dependence; in other cases, they have not diversified and so have drawn their principal supplier into a local conflict and in the process perhaps exacerbated it. The cold war has come closer to Africa in the Somalia-Ethiopia-Kenya, Congo-Zaire, Mali-Upper Volta, Uganda-Kenya, Angola-Zaire, Chad-Libya, and Algeria-Morocco/Mauritania conflicts in this way. In most cases, of course, the effect of such "guilt by association" has not been of catastrophic proportions for many of the arms suppliers, but it has been an unnecessary hindrance to their relations with the other African side without gaining the supplier any decisive advantage beyond the immediate moment with the countries they supplied.

Obviously, however, policy on arms sales must be decided case by case. A blanket moratorium is difficult to apply in such a diverse area, and yet several aspects of the notion are worth considering. First, even if a unilateral moratorium is too narrow or too tight, a general policy of lessened arms sales should be lobbied among Western arms suppliers and African purchasers alike. The events of 1977 showed rather clearly that the United States does not support South Africa with arms and that it does support an atom-free Africa. The clarity of this position should help remove a rationale for arming the other African states. Second, restraint in arms sales to Africa should become the subject of détente discussions. The ouster of the Soviets from Somalia, coming on the heels of similar reverses in Sudan and Egypt, should be used to convince them of the transience of relationships bought with arms and of the value of limiting escalatory arms sales. Third, an active attempt to help resolve specific disputes that underlie arms requests should also be part of American policy. Such attempts need not and generally should not take the form of direct mediation, but rather should lie in the area of good offices, discreet suggestions, and pressure to use more relevant third parties like the OAU.

The Carter administration began its term with similar views

on arms supplies to Africa but appears rapidly to have moved away from them. After sending Zaire only spare parts and Coca-Cola during the Shaba invasion (and leaving more direct support to Morocco, an African country, and logistic support to France), it then began discussions with Somalia, which already has the "best trained and equipped army in Africa," and agreed to "consider sympathetically" any military request from Chad, and prepared to sell anti-guerrilla material to Morocco. Yet after having made such positive responses and raised hopes, the United States then pulled back, delivering no arms but also doing nothing to help solve the basic conflicts. The United States, may thus have contributed to evicting Russia from a valuable military position in Somalia, but it has not tried to contribute measurably to a solution for the bitter feud in the Horn or for the dismemberment of Ethiopia, or for the undeclared war in the Western Sahara.

Africa at the end of the 1970s stands at a turning point where military conquest, so long beyond the norms of inter-African relations, may suddenly become a conceivable option. It will require major contributions from many quarters to prevent this, including not only restraint in arms sales but also diplomatic support for territorial stability and diplomatic inventiveness in finding nonmilitary solutions. The United States should not be the policeman in such a situation nor should it be the gunshop, but to avoid those roles it should be prepared to proffer innovative good offices or serve less formally but equally constructively as a catalyst.

II. Sources of Conflict

Four different sources of conflict are present in the normal evolution of African politics and development: problems of elite succession, problems of national consolidation, problems of subregional cooperation, and problems of foreign alliance.

1. Important leadership changes are due in Africa, both at the top and at the supporting levels. For a number of reasons, new elites will move into power, in some cases as early as the present decade. First, 19 states are still ruled by the Independence Generation (the "Class of 1918" by the average birth year of their heads of state), which is not only getting old, but in some cases has stood as an obstacle to promotion for younger, better trained, differently thinking successors. (Some of these states will be discussed below.) The Independence Generation has not only occupied the political structures of states but has also dominated their politics, with rivalries that originated in the pre-independence period often continuing well into the independent years.

Second, the military interlude also raises problems of succession. The Military Generation (the military arm of the "Class of 1931" by the same measure) came to power because the Independence Generation was unable to meet the inflated demands which it created, and frequently—notably in Algeria, Benin, Ghana, Nigeria, Uganda, Sudan and Zaire—because its energies were dissipated in pursuing its pre-independence rivalries. In those 20 countries where it has been tried, the Military Generation will wear thin, as both sides become aware of the fact that the military is no better governor than are civilians; this is already happening, in various ways, in Nigeria, Ghana, Upper Volta, Uganda, and Algeria. The military will have accomplished one important thing, however: the removal of the Independence Generation and the preparation for the entry of a new generation into politics and government. In those countries which have not yet undergone the military interlude, military rule is a potential alternative if the necessary causes are present, as they may be in Mauritania, Kenya, Sierra Leone, or other states.

Third, the phenomenon of "critical realignments" in political sentiment and public issues operates in Africa as elsewhere, providing new policy concerns, new supporting socio-political coalitions and new attitudes that change in waves and bunches rather than gradually. Political independence, symbolic equality with the metropole, cold war dichotomies, African political unity, nationalist single-party mobilization, and other paramount issues of the 1960s have given way to other concerns, such as economic self-reliance, authenticity, economic compensation and equity, North-South dichotomies, subregional cooperation, managerial efficiency, and others. The Great Coalition of traditional and modern elites which combined under a nationalist banner to strive for independence is breaking up as socio-political pluralism begins to develop—in some cases to the point of carrying with it competing policy options.

Despite such common characteristics and attitudes among the coming political generation, these elements can add up to two very different types for the "Class of 1945." On one hand, there is the Civic Generation, well-educated, combining traits of the leadership types of Politician and Technician, oriented toward order and efficiency, national production for national consumption, national identity, and modernization; these are often impatient with the South African problem as a diversion from development. On the other hand, there is the Militant Generation, with the same education and leadership traits, but oriented toward rapid decoupling, aggressively confrontationist on North-South issues, xenophobic and authentistic, viewing the struggle in South Africa as the last opportunity for a military victory of African colonized over colonizer.

In fact, these two apparently antithetical types are two sides of the same African nationalist coin, but characterized by

[99]

Westerners as "the kind we can talk to" and "the kind we can't." One is pragmatic, the other ideological, reflecting a return to the same split that divided Africa in the late 1950s and early 1960s. Positive awareness and shared concern in the West over issues of African self-reliance and liberation can help keep this generation of leaders from moving from a diplomatic to a confrontationist stage. Both self-reliance and liberation are watershed issues. Unless real progress is shown on both fronts—progress, moreover, that is possible in the current context—the pragmatic, realistic generation may be submerged by the ideologues.

Seven African states pose special problems of elite succession, since their heads of state are aged 70 or over: Kenya: Kenyatta (b. '92); Swaziland: Sobhuza II (b. '99); Tunisia: Bourguiba (b. '03); Ivory Coast: Houphouet-Boigny (b. '05); Sierra Leone: Stevens (b. '05); Malawi: Banda (b. '06); and Senegal: Senghor (b. '07). While in Swaziland, Tunisia and Malawi the chief of state holds office for life, other states held recent elections or are scheduled to do so soon (Senegal in 1978, Kenya in 1979, Ivory Coast in 1980, Sierra Leone in 1981) and either a successor will be elected or the national "George Washington" himself will run in order to hand over power during his reign. In all cases, there are younger generations waiting in the wings; and in most cases, the succession is likely to involve more of a change in supporting elites than occurred in other recent instances of normal succession, in Gabon, Morocco, and Liberia. It would take a full study on each case to do justice to the topic, but a few observations can be attempted here.

In cases where there is an established political structure, an active incumbent social group, and general economic growth, such as Tunisia, Ivory Coast, Kenya, Swaziland, and possibly Senegal (despite poor economic performance), a smooth

[100]

succession and policy continuity may be expected, although a gradual change in the favorable attitudes now held toward the metropole—or, in the Swazi case, toward South Africa—is certain. In all cases, the system is legitimized and controlled above all by a strong and more or less charismatic George Washington figure, whose shoes it will be impossible to fill. In some cases, like Ivory Coast, Swaziland and Senegal, and perhaps Sierra Leone and Malawi, where there is no major personal and policy challenge outside the system, the president's entourage can provide a successor and a collective leadership that will have a good chance of maintaining continuity and stability. In all of these cases, however, there are roles to fill—clear policy alternatives, disfavored ethnic causes—that can provide the opportunity for a counter-elite spokesman if economic conditions should worsen and payoff resources become scarce. In two cases—Malawi and Swaziland—the policy context has changed completely with the independence of Mozambique, providing an additional horse to ride if the currently successful policies of absorbing the opposition run out of resources. In a few cases, however, such as Kenya, Sierra Leone, and perhaps Senegal, the infighting of succession may so threaten stability that the state may end up on the list of African military regimes. Only in Tunisia and Senegal is there a strong likelihood of a competitive or bi- or multi-party system growing out of the nationalist movement and providing stable alternance of power, but in this business there are no certainties.

Overall, however, with the exception of the accommodationist policies of Malawi and perhaps Swaziland, the general policy directions established in these seven states and the general structure of their societies are likely to stand. None of these states or societies is ripe for a revolution—red, green, or whatever—and even a military regime would be expected to want to restore political order to encourage economic growth. Such growth orientations may be tempered by increased concern for distribution but not as a major policy change. The argument, therefore, is for a certain degree of stability in the political system of most of these states and thus for some of the political conditions conducive to growth and well-being. Given a choice or a chance to exert influence, Americans doubtless find such systems more compatible and hospitable to work with than the less stable or more ideological ones, although we should also learn to work with ideological regimes as well (as discussed below).

2. With rare exceptions, the African state is still neither a territorial state nor a nation-state. That is, the political writ still does not run to the finite boundaries of a country, nor are its inhabitants wrapped up in one common overriding sense of identity. Added to this fact is the further problem inherent in the existence of a number of "non-viable" states, sovereign countries short on people or place. More specifically, there are three kinds of problems associated with national consolidation: the mega-state, the large multinational territory in danger of falling apart; the mini-state, the tiny country coveted by the neighbor; and the unsettled or disputed boundary. Before turning to an example, let it be noted that, in general, African states large and small are likely to hold together and defend their fragile sovereignty far better than their inchoate nature might suggest but that boundaries are likely to be far more frequent subjects of dispute than the OAU consensus on their unalterable nature might lead one to believe.

National consolidation is clearly in American, as well as African, interest. National disintegration, irredentism, and an absence of national identity create the very problems of instability which draw in hasty great-power involvement in crisis, forcing interventions which may be even more destabilizing, based on judgments of interests taken at the most difficult time. If development for the better welfare of the citizens is in the interest of Africans and also in the interest of a United States looking for strong self-reliant societies, then national disintegration and territorial disputes are costly distractions. Furthermore, although it would be hard to claim that any African state—or perhaps any state anywhere—has the perfect size, shape and contents, it is certain that the interests of stability and development are not served by more and smaller national units. Indeed, it is hard to claim even that individual cases should be judged on their merits, since the merits of any single case set precedents for other less meritorious instances. Wisely, this was the point of view adopted in Washington in the Katangan war, the Biafran war, and the southern Sudanese rebellion, and it is a sound principle to apply to subsequent cases. The only value served by a contrary policy would be the abstract principle of national self-determination itself, a dangerous Pandora's box unless restricted—as usually interpreted currently—to state-national units.

None of this prevents a positive policy of negotiated boundary rectifications and territorial exchanges or regional integration among neighboring units. To begin with, African states in general should be encouraged to delineate and demarcate their boundaries as soon as possible, before state jurisdictions conflict and border disputes arise. Most undemarcated boundaries are in two areas: in the Sahara, and between states formerly under the same colonial ruler: e.g., the borders of Algeria; of Cameroon, Niger, Benin and Chad (except with Nigeria); of the Central African Empire (except with Zaire); of Mali and Sudan. It is a meticulous technical matter to put up boundary markers, but it is cheaper than war.

African states should also be encouraged to negotiate

mutually satisfactory boundaries when the inherited line can be improved. The landmark case that has received too little attention is the 1963 boundary rectification negotiated between Mauritania and Mali in order to overcome some problems of supply for nomads, the only such boundary change negotiated between independent states in Africa. A number of other areas could benefit from such treatment, beginning with the Ethiopian Ogaden and the Moroccan Sahara, and it would be a mark of statesmanship for the United States to encourage it. The matter of regional integration is discussed in the next section, but first some specific cases of national consolidation need examination.

As a case of all three problems, Ethiopia is in deep trouble. Whereas other states are held together by an absence of alternatives, Ethiopia is plagued by territorial rebellions that its neighbors are eager to support, notably in the Ogaden, disputed areas along the Sudanese border to the west, and the separatist territory of Eritrea on the northeast. In between, the newly independent mini-state of Djibouti is part of Somalia irredenta while at the same time serving as the railhead for Adis Ababa's lifeline. A number of other provinces in Ethiopia itself have also had serious revolts in the 1970s, without direct international ramifications. Historically restive under Amhara (Ethiopian) imperial rule, these various regions seized upon the breakdown of central authority brought about by the Ethiopian revolution of the mid-1970s to break away from domination by Addis Ababa.

Most of Ethiopia's centrifugal revolts are not the new nationalist stirrings of a multinational empire, but rather the vestigial reactions of a feudal "federation" to modernizing centralization and then to a collapse of central authority: Vendées not Biafras. While it is unlikely that many of these provincial revolts will end in anything but a more or less temporary breakdown in authority, the revolts in the two eastern Muslim areas could end in secession, leaving Ethiopia two-thirds smaller and landlocked. In these two cases, the rebellions are part of a longer historical process of conflict between Christian Amharic Ethiopia and its Muslim neighbors, reinforced in the south by the relentless demographic pressure of the expanding Somali nation.

Neither Sudan's nor Ethiopia's well-being is enhanced by an independent Eritrea; and although Eritrea is Ethiopia's most developed province, even the Eritreans would not necessarily be better off in their own independent state. The same is true with regard to Ogaden and Somalia, but it does seem that in more peaceful times a more satisfactory boundary could be found if the national aspirations of the Somalis living in Ogaden (Ethiopia's least developed province) could be determined without upsetting the OAU boundary conventions. The fate of Djibouti is equally complicated. The territory is likely to be the subject of a move to join Somalia within a few years, either from inside or from outside. The ethnic Somalis (Issas) live in the southern part of the state and Djibouti city; the Ethiopian-related peoples (Afars) live in the north.

Were its internal troubles not cultivated by its neighbors, Ethiopia could simply "drop out" of international politics for a while until it had set the provincial rooms of its house in order and worked out the degree of revolution it is prepared to sustain. Since this is not possible, the Horn of Africa will continue to be a conflict area. There is no American advantage to a dismembered Ethiopia, and a good deal of instability will result from a proliferation of new, weak, poor states in the region. Given the continuing conflict potential of this type of situation, this instability is unlikely to be outweighed by the eviction of the Russians from their Somali bases when considered from the viewpoint of the interests of the West.

[105]

The famous Pandora's box of inherited boundaries will have been opened, and a precedent set either for the alteration of frontiers and annexation of territory by force among independent African states or for the open use of foreign armies to restore the status quo. None of the resulting entities will be a more "natural" or "viable" state as a result.

At best, the passage of time could lead to a stalemate which might be followed by outside proposals for the solution of the conflict. One such proposal could be to encourage a settlement that would trade part of Ogaden (to Somalia) for Djibouti (to Ethiopia). Another would be to support a division of Djibouti along ethnic lines and to provide the necessary aid to build a new railroad roughly alongside the Addis-Assab road to Tajura/Obock on the northern shore of the bay (including new port facilities at the railhead). The bay is deepest toward the north shore and protected by the mountains, with passes and terrain appropriate for a roadbed. Djibouti itself might then be an empty prize, or, if it were not, at least it could be kept under surveillance from across the bay.

Ethiopia is the "hot case" of 1977-78, but other states face the same problems. It is no accident that the prime examples are the large states of the continent, including most of the other subregional giants. Zaire and Nigeria, the dominant states in central and west Africa, by their very size in area and population encompass enough diverse ethnic groups to contain the potential for disintegration; and Sudan, somewhat less of a subregional power although Africa's largest state in area, is in the same position. In each case the potential has had its example in recent history, the Katanga and Shaba revolts (successive names for the same province) in Zaire, the Biafran war in Nigeria, the southern secession in Sudan. In none of these three cases is there an open boundary problem like Ethiopia's with Somalia, and in none is there the compounding

[106]

problem of a mini-state—unless one includes the Angolan enclave of Cabinda, separated from the main territory and coveted by Zaire.

The political history of Nigeria since independence in 1960 can be interpreted as a succession of models for intrastate relations among a number of single-party states. Initially, there was a "balance of power" within a federal framework, a system of shifting alliances among the three constituent single-party states. By the time of the 1964 elections, like many balance-of-power systems, the Nigerian pattern of relations had broken down into a bipolar system, with the dominant side then seeking the elimination of the other coalition. The result—again as often happens in international relations—was war, and an attempt to base relations on independent units, the solution posed by Biafra. The response to secession—again as frequently occurs—was finally a centralized system: first with a warlord arrangement for governing the increased number of provinces under Gowon, and then with a more articulated arrangement of administrators and assemblies over a further increased number of provinces under Obasanjo and the new constitution. The larger number of provincial units, the reasserted central authority, and the unpleasant experience with the previous systems, coupled with the increased resources from oil out of which to meet the demands of the participants in the political system, all work to make the present arrangement more stable than its predecessors. It is this prospect of stability and of the progress which accompanies it that underlies the increasingly active role of Nigeria in foreign policy and its evolving cooperation with the United States on matters of mutual concern.

For all the violence and bitterness created by the Biafran war, which paralyzed African international relations for three years, Nigeria has had a number of factors working toward national consolidation. Its new oil wealth permits payoffs and rewards to loyal participants in the political system; its absence of predatory neighbors reduces support for local secessionist movements; its overwhelming weight—the largest population, total GNP, and army in Africa—discourages venturesome opponents; and its legitimacy as a federal state in West Africa, where balkanization has been so frequently criticized, makes it an unlikely scapegoat.

Zaire has not been so fortunate. Its attempts at national consolidation have reflected a series of experiments similar to Nigeria's although less formalized: a provincial balance of power, attempts at a centralized state, more frequent attempts at secession, and finally a patron-client system of political control from the center by promotion-demotion *(shumshir* to use the Ethiopian term for the classical imperial control device) and payoffs. But Zaire's communications infrastructure is in poor condition to permit centralized control; it has a constant history of bad relations with its two western neighbors, Congo and Angola, and sporadic conflicts with Sudan, Uganda, and Tanzania to the east; and it was born as an independent state in an ideological dispute that has left its regime, whatever it may be, under a pall of questionable legitimacy ever since.

Zaire's most recent troubles were typical examples of ineptitude and vulnerability. When President Mobutu, despite an agreement with Angolan President Neto, was unable or unwilling to curb the remnant bands of the defeated Angolan nationalist factions along the border, Angola twice unleashed restive groups of Katangan opponents to Mobutu's regime who had taken refuge in Angola. The 1977 invasion of Shaba (Katanga) was condemned by the African states when finally taken to the OAU, three weeks after its outbreak, but it was welcomed by the many Zairois exile groups as the first step toward the overthrow of the Mobutu regime. At home, Mobutu used the invasion as an excuse to rid himself of his closest lieutenant and Foreign Minister, Nguzu Karl-I Bond, on the pretext that he had failed to pass on a warning of the threat. Both times Moroccan and French support gave the needed assistance to the Zairois army, which has received large quantities of American arms. The United States has developed a shakily close relationship with the Mobutu regime as the best of all available alternatives, with a better record for holding the state together than for making it move.

Sudan—and all the other states westward to Mauritania along the shatter zone between black and Arab populations—has a single ethnic division rather than the pluralistic disintegration threatened in other states. The southern rebellion may be dated from the military mutiny of 1955, before independence, and, after a civilian parliamentary interlude, was responsible for the overthrow both of the conservative military government in the mini-revolution of 1964 and then of the new civilian government in the radical military coup of 1969. The problem was settled by an agreement on southern autonomy in 1972 and has remained quiescent since then.

The reverse problem exists next door in Chad, where a rebellion by the Arab minority in the north has occupied the government since independence and eventually led to a military overthrow; the French have supported the government and Libya has intervened militarily in support of the rebellion. As the Sudanese experience has shown, such rebellions are beyond a purely military solution and can be resolved only by political means in addition to military pressure. Problems of terrain, communication, limited resources, and some admittedly legitimate grievances against the national distributive process hamper efforts to eradicate the rebellions and make some accommodation necessary.

[109]

It is impossible to predict where the next outbreak of resistance against national consolidation will occur. Whenever the constraints of consolidation are felt to outweigh the benefits, local populations will resist to protect their previous autonomy; whenever the benefits of modernization are unequally distributed, to the flagrant neglect of a group that can rally around a common identity, they will take to the hills to demand more benefits or less interference. These rebellions could then occur anywhere. It is in the common interest of the African country and of the United States (whatever its attitude toward the particular regime, a complicating consideration) to smooth out these inevitable bumps on the road to national consolidation. But how to do so is less evident. Sometimes it requires adequate military supplies, sometimes an extra increment of some resource to balance the benefits, sometimes a bit of political advice or pressure to equalize the domestic distribution of payoffs. The last is cheapest but most delicate.

3. While pursuing national consolidation, African states also pursue unity in the form of subregional cooperation, although in the process they have learned that the first is a precondition to the second. If the OAU system has been singularly unsuccessful in handling the "upper" and "lower" ranges of inter-African policy—liberation and internal war—it has heretofore been effective in the "middle ranges" of conflict and cooperation among African states. Conflict management and even conflict resolution have been carried out within the concert system, and an impressive list of subregional groups have maintained a modest level of coordinated services—the Central African Economic and Customs Union (UDEAC), Council of the Entente, river and lake basin groups, to mention a few.

Beneath these institutions is the trend toward increasing subregional interactions: In all subregions, diplomatic exchanges (missions and visits) have been higher than at the continental level, and in west, central and southern Africa the number of official visits within the region has doubled every four years over the past decade. By another measure, although inter-African trade is not high, almost all of the pairs of African states whose trade with each other is greater than 5 percent of their total trade are drawn from the same subregion. Other indicators could be added to show the slowly growing trend of subregionalization.

Two subregions have particular problems that are both important in and of themselves and are typical of other areas. The Economic Community of West African States (ECOWAS/CEDEAO) was established in November 1976 and so far has run into no more specific problems than the general difficulty of bringing states in the region together. As in the case of other attempts at economic cooperation in West Africa, ineffectiveness may be the price of durability. "Going it alone" to preserve fragile sovereignty and inchoate institutions, and "fighting it out" to pursue sentimental and commercial rivalries are the two greatest competitors of West African cooperation. The interest shown by Nigeria, Ghana, and Ivory Coast, however, is likely to outweigh the rivalries of Senegal and Guinea, if they remain in, and to overcome the gap between French- and English-speakers.

On the other side of the continent, the troubles of the East African Economic Community are essentially a result of its three members' efforts at fighting it out and going it alone. Two other problems not found in West Africa—the offensive presence of Idi Amin and the juxtaposition of two antithetical socio-economic regimes in archetypical form in the two other

[111]

states—are exacerbated by the fact that the Community is limited to these three members. It may be better to start all over again.

The states of southeast Africa are more closely tied together by common transportation, energy, and labor networks than are the states of the East African Community; and their regimes, for all their differences, may be at least less openly antagonistic than Kenya's and Tanzania's. Cooperation, of course, has as its precondition the independence of Zimbabwe; but once this has occurred, a Zambesi Group of Zambia, Zimbabwe, Malawi, Mozambique, and Tanzania makes sense. Tanzania has already (in 1977) begun to make such arrangements with Mozambique. Obviously, to build cooperation is not a rapid matter; and it may take its initial form only as bi- and multilateral conventions, ad hoc visits and meetings, and joint government studies, and—on the very important level of attitudes—a positive view of cooperation and a willingness to avoid finding one's own national identity through negative comparisons with one's neighbors.

A proper and useful policy attitude by an outside great power toward subregional cooperation is a rather delicate matter. The reticence of the African states themselves, the fact that the United States cannot oblige others to cooperate, and the fact that American diplomatic representatives are accredited to states, not to regions, militates against an effective policy here. Yet on the American as well as the African side, there is much in an attitude. Business branches and investments can be encouraged to look for a subregional rather than simply a national market when they enter an African country. More important, business can take more positive or aggressive advantage of existing subregional arrangements rather than follow the defensive strategy of market organization or segmentation so often adopted thus far. Embassies, or at least their commercial and even political sections, can be instructed to coordinate and communicate subregionally. A revival of an earlier focus of American policy on subregional or cooperative projects of benefit to several African states would be a useful addition to aid criteria. Above all, one must recognize that subregional cooperation can only succeed if it is a positive-sum proposition: not simply an exercise in redistribution whereby some receive more than they would on their own but at the expense of others, but rather a creative construction enabling all partners to do better than they would alone even if they benefit unequally. Attention to an experiment such as ECO-WAS in these terms may provide opportunities for useful assistance as well as encouragement as the occasions arise, and save the Community from following the example of East Africa or of previous West African attempts at cooperation.

4. The African continent is an open field of opportunities and traps for foreign powers, and particularly for the United States. It should be noted that there would be nothing but traps if the southern African conflict turned to revolution and an OAU-Pretoria war. In that case, the United States would probably not live up to African desires and would suffer badly in its African relations, probably losing influence elsewhere in the world as well, to a greater degree than in the Vietnam War. The manner in which Zimbabwe attains independence is crucial to the political direction of southern Africa, a negotiated (political) transition providing a more "moderate" member of the southern region than a guerrilla (military) takeover. On the other hand, the revolution in South Africa has already begun and will render increasingly difficult the search for *interlocuteurs valables* should the government ever decide on meaningful reforms.

This said, however, African states have much to gain from good relations with outside powers, and there are few African

[113]

states which do not have specific advantages—in terms of their own national interest—to gain from close relations with the United States. It is therefore on the other side of the relationship that questions should be posed: How close should relations be, and with whom?

To the first question, it seems that there are no imperatives that make particular African states absolutely necessary or unnecessary to U.S. foreign policy interests. The strongest strategic concern is the need to prevent hostile bases on shores or transportation routes of importance to the United States, not the positive need for American presence on those routes and shores. Traditional friendships and concentrated investments are important but flexible matters.

One conclusion then is the importance of avoiding too close relations with countries that are not vital to American interests. The other conclusion is that there is no need to use inter-African conflicts and even ideological tendencies (notably in the case of the newly independent "radical" states) as a reason for avoiding good relations. By the same token, there is no need to be stuck with any particular African ally through the thick and thin of its inter-African conflicts, since—as has been seen—common interests do not run deeply enough between the United States and African states to provide the basis for an alliance. This realization may not be very comforting to African regimes but is consistent both with reality and with most states' notions of nonalignment, and it leaves the United States freer to concentrate on projects and interests rather than on obligations. What then should be the criteria for American interest in Africa, particularly in relation to coming political problems?

Many criteria have been proposed. The first error would be to take any of them exclusively. For example, observers have noted that, to obtain maximum cooperation and effectiveness, a foreign program of support should strengthen and not undermine the position of the receiving regime. Yet as a single criterion this guideline would provide a recipe for guaranteed corruption. Another school looks for friends, finding in a recent history of support for Zaire's Mobutu or Ethiopia's late Haile Selassie or Kenya's Kenyatta or Morocco's Hassan or Tunisia's Bourguiba a relationship akin to deeper historical ententes such as with England, France, Canada, or even Lebanon or Israel. Friendship facilitates cooperation, as long as it lasts, but it is not a justification for support in the absence of longer and deeper interests in common. To act otherwise is to confuse cause and effect.

Yet criteria, particularly for economic aid, are necessary. Even as rich a power as the United States cannot support all the projects and fill all the requests of needy African states. Policy requires that choices be made, and the suggestion that choice among states as worthily needy as those of Africa smacks of triage simply misunderstands the nature of the policy process. Thus, another school proposes need as a criterion for support in Africa. Appealing, and obvious, as the criterion may sound, it leads to curious conclusions. Either it provides no criterion at all, as has been suggested, since Africa's need is so great and widespread; or else it gives rise to a purely remedial policy, allowing the poorest states to catch up with the poor. There is much of this dilemma in the crash programs of disaster relief, notably those in relief of the initial Sahel famine; it is not callous to question the wisdom of policies that rush to alleviate the effects of disaster only to give growing populations a new lease on poverty. Remedial criteria certainly respond to a need but not effectively. The Sahel Club's 1978-82 development program also responds to need, but on a sounder preventive basis.

Ideological criteria have also been proposed. They may

include favorable votes in the United Nations, or support on key specific policies (such as Vietnam) or for favored types of political and developmental systems. Vote-buying is ephemeral, and creates a situation where the other party is actually being trained to ask what has been done for it lately. Support for particular types of political systems would not be as unreasonable if the correlation between system-type and results were firmly established. As it is, although some types of systems are obviously counterproductive or beyond the pale of justice, it has not yet been proven whether an African socialist or African bourgeois system, or a single-party or multi-party regime, provides the better developmental results, or, for that matter, at what point the exam should be given. Again, to seek criteria in political systems is to mistake effect for cause.

Two other criteria are more serious competitors. One calls for projects to be judged on their own merits, including the chances of effective realization in the host country. Project criteria are crucial; the question is whether they alone should be determinant. No one would argue for the selection of projects that could not be accomplished or would be ineffective in their impact, although sometimes projects are judged in the abstract rather than having their chances of effectiveness assessed beforehand. Among project criteria, important distinctions could be pursued: between remedial and developmental, or building and training, or other types of projects. Yet beyond these questions—which will not be argued here—is the broader question of country criteria.

Whatever development projections and philosophies are chosen, the picture of industrial and pre-industrial worlds gradually pulling apart across a developmental gap is only partially true. It is more accurate to note that while some states are both underdeveloped and underdeveloping, others in the Third World are pulling ahead. Not only do they show significant growth rates; they have a sizable total GNP, a growing resource base to feed a leadership capability in the continent and the Third World, an expanding education system, a possibility of absorbing greater numbers of their own population into the modern socio-economic (and political) sector, and eventually a chance of "making it" into the concert of industrial powers, as originally the United States, then Japan, then China, Turkey and Iran and others have added themselves to the European center of world politics. A number of African states are part of this process; Algeria and Nigeria are destined for a role of significance; some states—such as Kenya, Ivory Coast, Ghana, Cameroon, Congo, Morocco, Tunisia—are on the road to gradually extending the advantages of the modernized sector to the entire population; and there are strong possibilities for successful development in southern Africa. A survey of African growth rates shows that even a decade from now, eleven states—Ethiopia, Somalia, Sudan, Rwanda, Burundi, Upper Volta, Mali, Guinea, Niger, Benin, Chad—will not have achieved a per capita GNP of more than $150. But there are another ten states—Nigeria, Morocco, Cameroon, Ivory Coast, Congo, Angola, Mozambique, Swaziland, Zimbabwe, Botswana—which will have a per capita GNP between $500 and $900, and five more over $1,000— South Africa, Tunisia, Libya, Algeria, and Gabon. The United States should be particularly interested in those countries which have the resources and the policies to proceed with their own development and expand their modernization. It should be concerned that they not only continue to show growth but also continue to absorb new elements into the modernized sector, developing the creative energies that we believe come with social pluralism and political competition. These are the societies which will be gradually able to take care of their own poor and help others. As they grow in

[117]

strength, they will either try to lead the poorer countries in revolt against the world system or will try to join it themselves. It is the latter policy which should be encouraged, and this encouragement can be the major thrust of U.S. policy.

Such a policy approach has been criticized for being elitist, inhumane, offensive, and impolitic. In part, the accusation of elitism has some truth if it refers to the most effective users of aid and political support. If it is elitist to help polities with the greatest—though still insufficient—capacity for helping themselves and with the best promise of using the aid effectively, then it is elitism well placed. Conversely, in schematic terms, it is doubtless more inhumane to spread too little too thin than it is to provide a few with barely enough. Relief aid is a response of world brotherhood and there will continue to be emergency funds and appeals for it; but it is not a foreign policy. The idea that states will consider it offensive to be chosen as "most likely to succeed" by the United States and hence worthy of aid and support, or that they may perceive in American help an attempt to co-opt them into a community of our making, denies their proven capacity for political independence and the realities of history as well. Throughout history, the new states which have entered into the world concert have shown a remarkable capacity for retaining their goals and making an impact on their co-optors. The alternative is perpetual exclusion, quite the contrary of the goals of developing societies.

The political criticism is more realistic but incomplete. As an exclusive declared policy, to concentrate attention on a few states alone would be the first step in the division of the continent into a zone of satisfaction and a zone of unrest, and the gratuitous handing over of the latter to any other power which would adopt it. Several bridges can be thrown across these lines. The subregional groupings discussed above can help with the coordination and distribution of benefits from stronger leaders to needier neighbors. Emergency and even ongoing philanthropic attention to some broad problems will still be required; the Sahel disaster is not over, nor are the efforts to improve local capabilities for confronting it. Multilateral aid—in the material sense, but also in trade provisions—can be expected to pay greater attention to weaker economies.

It would be too much to say that American policy toward the continent in the past—again, with the exception of southern Africa—has been "bankrupt" or a "failure," as is sometimes alleged. But the future brings important changes and new political conflicts in Africa, and guidelines for foreseeing and meeting them should be considered beforehand. It is unrealistic to think that choice is unnecessary; and if there is to be choice, criteria are needed. A mixed criterion involving project effectiveness, African dedication in attacking the country's own problems, and a promise of growth and stability within the country can be a useful basis for allocating American support and developing closer relations. Thereafter, other principles can be added, such as respect for human rights, cooperation in the subregion, maintenance of territorial stability, and others, by which specific events can be judged. In a word, a pragmatic policy is called for, one that signals American concern for projects, policies, and countries according to their ability and willingness to produce results, whatever the political color of the regime. Such a policy will be useful in maximizing support and effort, and in showing recipients and observers alike that aid and assistance go with independence and self-reliance, not with dependence and clients.

FOUR

U.S. Strategic Interests and Military Options in Sub-Saharan Africa

Geoffrey Kemp

Sub-Saharan Africa has become a region of increasing strategic importance to the United States, primarily because of its geographic position vis-à-vis two critical theaters, the North Atlantic and the Middle East-Persian Gulf. The United States also has considerable strategic interests in access to African mineral wealth. In addition, this country faces policy dilemmas concerning arms sales to black African countries and possibly military intervention in the event of crises on the subcontinent. Because certain U.S. strategic interests do not necessarily coincide with political, economic or even ideological interests, there is some controversy over the relative importance which should be attached to strategic and military considerations in formulating a cohesive U.S. policy toward Africa.

Africa's crises, and issues therein for the United States, have been escalating in number and intensity in the last several years. The introduction of Soviet and Cuban equipment and manpower into Angola, Ethiopia, and possibly Uganda has caused concern in the United States, Latin America, Europe, and the Middle East. The crises in Rhodesia and Uganda created by black and white racist regimes pose difficulties for the United States as it attempts to redefine its African policy and yet avoid becoming directly embroiled in the ongoing conflicts in that region. In the Horn of Africa there is confusion, with the United States now ousted from the facilities of its former ally, Ethiopia, and the Soviet Union ejected from Somalia and the base at Berbera—while the Soviets and Cubans pour military aid into Ethiopia and the Somalis importune the United States for arms and aid. (Meanwhile, to some extent Saudi Arabia has moved in to fill the aid gap in Somalia.)

For the future, the question of U.S. relations with South Africa may become a major issue in U.S. domestic politics. Although there have been numerous internal disturbances in South Africa over the past years, the basic strength of the white regime is much greater than has been the case in Rhodesia, and, therefore, on the assumption that there will be no immediate resolution of the conflict, one can expect a protracted, perhaps deteriorating situation.

In addition to these local factors, broad changes are occurring in the world's strategic environment which, in turn, influence the importance of Africa. These changes have resulted in what can only be described as a new strategic map.[1] The new strategic map is made up of four components: (1) the diffusion of political, economic and military power to the less-industrial world; (2) the increasing importance of resource interdependency for the Western industrial world,

[121]

the Communist countries, and the less-industrial countries; (3) the changing patterns of Western and Soviet basing rights throughout the world, in particular in the Indo-Pacific region and the Mediterranean; and (4) the new laws of the sea which are drastically altering the map of the world's oceans, seaways, and choke-points.

In the context of Western strategic interests, one effect of the new map is to highlight the role of the southern seas in Western strategy, namely, the Indian Ocean-South Atlantic region covering an area from the Persian Gulf, southern Africa, West Africa, to the coast of Brazil, and the line from the Caribbean to the Mediterranean. Within this region the major part of the West's oil flows to Europe and North America. So long as this oil remains vital to Western economic and military power, threats to its security—whether land threats, political threats, economic threats, or threats from the sea—must be taken seriously. Current projections are that for at least the next ten years oil will remain vital, and, therefore, the Indian Ocean environment, and to a lesser extent events in the South Atlantic, must now be carefully examined within a Western strategic context. It is this factor, together with the increased Soviet maritime presence in the region, which points to the *new* geographical importance of sub-Saharan Africa.

As a result of these events there are inevitable pressures for the United States to reassess its foreign policy toward the region. Alternative policies span a broad range: the exclusion of the Soviet Union from access to bases and facilities in Africa; support, including arms sales, for black regimes opposed to South Africa and Rhodesia; support for pro-West black regimes opposed to pro-Soviet radical regimes; support for South Africa and a few select countries in central Africa, such as Zaire and Kenya, on the grounds that they have high strategic importance and are pro-West with strong leadership.

[122]

Obviously, choices have to be made. Apart from the issue of U.S. policy toward South Africa, the most difficult problems may be black African requests for U.S. arms aid. Countries such as Kenya, Zaire, and possibly Zambia can make a plausible argument for re-equipping their armed forces at a time when conflict is endemic throughout the region. Thus U.S. arms sales policy in Africa may become an increasingly important adjunct of a more positive diplomacy toward the region at the very time when the Carter administration has taken steps to reduce U.S. arms sales throughout the world.

One indispensable tool in resolving these dilemmas is a close examination of U.S. strategic interests in this area and the possible threats to them. Only after such an analysis has been undertaken, can we begin to judge how best to deal with potential threats. The purpose of this essay, therefore, will be to lay out the strategic situation facing the United States.

U.S. Strategic Interests

The strategic interests of the United States have two main aspects: first, the context of global strategy; and second, the context of military activities in sub-Saharan Africa itself, including arms sales and possible intervention.

In the event of a major war with the Soviet Union, Africa south of the Sahara has geographical importance in two ways. First, Soviet control or access to the ports, airfields, and support facilities in the bulge of West Africa and in the Horn of Africa would pose serious threats to the vital sea lines of communication between North America and western Europe to and from the Persian Gulf region. Second, Soviet control or access to major facilities in southern Africa, especially South Africa, would pose threats to the Cape route, which, in turn,

[123]

has direct military importance for the West and is also an extremely important sea route for maritime commerce. A third factor, not to be discounted, pertains to the strategic mineral resources located on the African continent, access to which could not be guaranteed were hostile powers to control or threaten them.

The geographical interests are by far the most important; and in this context the preferred U.S. goal is not so much to control the logistical facilities of Africa, although this would have obvious benefits, but rather to *deny* the Soviet Union such control. No other power poses a similar level of threat to the West. A Chinese presence in central Africa or the Horn would seem more competitive with the Soviet Union than with the West, and the Cuban contingents should be viewed in the context of overall Soviet global strategy.

We have already noted the importance of the new strategic map and its implications for Africa. Historically, however, there is nothing new in the thesis that the geography of sub-Saharan Africa, especially West Africa, the Horn, and the Cape routes, is important to the West. Throughout World War II, control of this area was considered essential to the Allies, and attempts were made by Japan and Germany to deny the Allies this control. The failure of both Germany and Japan to establish a major military presence in the region assured the West of secure lines of communication from theaters such as the Middle East, Latin America, and the Caribbean. The southern projection in the map shows, as our usual ethnocentric penchant for the traditional north-south Mercator projection serves to hide, the relative proximity of Latin America (in particular Brazil), Southern Africa, and Australia.

The Cape route has importance to the United States as a vital commercial sea lane for raw materials and as a route for

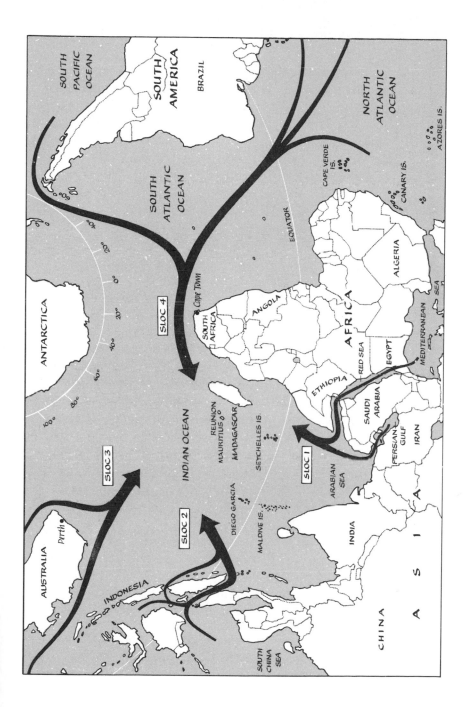

deploying maritime forces into the Indian Ocean-Persian Gulf region.[2] Regarding commercial shipping, the Cape route is one of the world's prime strategic sea lines of communication (SLOC) essentially because of the development of super-tankers which, originating in the Persian Gulf and traveling around the Cape, can deliver oil to Western ports at a price below that of smaller vessels transiting by way of the Suez Canal. Many other commodities, such as Zambian and Zairian copper and South African manganese, are also sent normally by way of the Cape route.

In using the term "Cape route," it is well to remember that this is merely a shorthand way of referring to several very large, very long, and *quite different* sea lines of communication tying the East to the West. The Cape route encompasses SLOCs linking Britain and the Far East, Nigeria and Japan, India and the United States, the Soviet Union and the Far East, and many other trading nations. The only unifying characteristic of these trade routes is that the products traded within each group travel for a part of their time off the coast of southern Africa. The amount of traffic around this area is high and shows every sign of remaining so despite the reopening of the Suez Canal. For instance, in 1966 approximately 500,000 barrels of oil per day transited the Cape. Today the figure is up to nearly 12,000,000 barrels of oil per day. On average, approximately a thousand ships other than oil tankers call per month at South Africa's four main ports: Cape Town, New London, Port Elizabeth and Durban.[3]

There are alternative peacetime routes for most of the products that are transported around the Cape. The Suez Canal could be used more, and eventually could be deepened to take some of the supertankers. Alternatively, supertankers can reach Europe and the eastern United States by way of the

[126]

Indonesian Straits or by sailing southeast across the Indian Ocean through the Bass Strait between Australia and Tasmania, across the bottom of the Southern Seas, through the Drake Passage and around Cape Horn, into the South Atlantic. They could also sail to western American ports and then be off-loaded onto smaller tankers and proceed through the Panama Canal to the U.S. eastern seaboard and to Europe. Most of these alternatives, however, would cost more in terms of time and would probably increase insurance rates.

Thus, in analyzing the strategic importance of commercial aspects of the Cape route, one has to take into account both *wartime* scenarios when alternatives could be found and more complicated *crisis* scenarios when the economic costs of not using the Cape route would, themselves, create serious economic problems for many members of the Western alliance and, indeed, many countries in the less developed world. If, for one reason or another, ships could not use the excellent facilities of the South African ports, undoubtedly the insurance rates would increase and, given the marginal profitability of many trading commodities, this could seriously affect the terms of trade for many of the primary producing countries of the region.

In terms of U.S. military interests, the Cape route is important as an entry into the Indian Ocean from the South Atlantic, and *vice versa*. Although the United States maintains a minimal naval presence of two escorts in the Indian Ocean, it does deploy a carrier task force into the area about three times a year. U.S. fleets are permanently stationed in the North Atlantic, the Mediterranean, and the East and West Pacific. In the event of a crisis in the Arabian Sea area, which includes the conflict regions of the Horn of Africa, the Persian Gulf, and South Asia, the United States has four major sea lines of

[127]

communication (SLOCs) along which it could deploy naval forces in an emergency.

SLOC 1: from the Mediterranean via the Suez Canal, Red Sea and Bab-el-Mandeb Strait, into the Arabian Sea;

SLOC 2: from the South and East China Seas and the Western Pacific through the Indonesian Strait, into the Indian Ocean;

SLOC 3: from the Western Pacific and China Seas around Southern Australia through the Bass Strait, into the Indian Ocean; and

SLOC 4: from the North Atlantic, and possibly from the Eastern Pacific via Cape Horn and/or Panama, through the South Atlantic, around the Cape of Good Hope, into the Indian Ocean.

SLOCs 1 and 2 are the shortest in distance but the most vulnerable in terms of physical and political constraints. The Suez Canal was blocked between 1967-75 and could very well be closed again in the event of another Arab-Israeli war. The Bab-el-Mandeb Strait at the mouth of the Red Sea is also very vulnerable and has been the site of several confrontations between Israel and the Arabs regarding shipping access. Hostile forces, including the Soviet Union, based in the People's Democratic Republic of Yemen or in the Horn of Africa, could close this strait to U.S. warships.

The SLOCs through the Indonesian Straits (Malacca, Sunda and Lombok) are *at present* more secure. But in view of the increasing economic activity in the area of the South China Sea, the potential for conflict between the littoral states over off-shore economic resources, and the claims by the Indonesians and Philippines to sovereignty over their entire archipelagos, it is easy to imagine a situation in which U.S. warships might not be permitted to pass through the Straits in a major crisis or would be placed under severe constraints.

SLOCs 3 and 4 are longer but have been more secure both geographically and politically. Due to the distances involved, the effective use of SLOCs 3 and 4 requires the frequent availability of oil for refueling the non-nuclear-powered ships of the U.S. fleets. There are four basic ways to reduce the fuel supply problem for the fleet: to use a nuclear-powered carrier task force; to use foreign bunkering facilities; to use oilers to support the fleet in transit; and to preposition U.S. oil supplies in forward bases.

The "ideal" solution is the first (although a nuclear-powered task force still needs aviation gas and ordnance), but the costs of building nuclear ships are astronomical, and given the lead-time required, the number of nuclear surface ships cannot grow very quickly. The most convenient option is the second, namely, to use local oil *en route.* However, it is not always the most secure, as was discovered during the 1973 Arab-Israeli war when the Saudi Arabian government put pressure on suppliers not to sell to the U.S. Navy. For the Cape route to the Indian Ocean, the traditional fuel stops from the North Atlantic and Mediterranean have included Bermuda, the Caribbean, Recife, Dakar, Luanda, Lourenço Marques (now Maputo), and Mombassa. A normal steam-powered destroyer needs to refuel about every three days if it is traveling in excess of 20 knots. If the black African facilities are denied and it were decided not to use South African ports, it would not be possible to deploy into the Indian Ocean without the use of oilers. New U.S. oilers (AOEs or fast combat-support ships as they are sometimes called) make it possible to sail into the Indian Ocean without using indigenous facilities and without seriously hampering the speed of transit.

[129]

In short, the oilers can get the fleet there. Problems begin to arise, however, once the fleet is on station and is required to participate in maneuvers or, if necessary, military actions. In this case, the oilers themselves need to be replenished; and although this is possible by using the many tankers available to the Navy and by chartering civilian merchant tankers, the costs go up greatly if oil is not available locally.

In fact, it would be difficult to imagine the U.S. Navy operating at high tempo for any period of time in the Indian Ocean area unless it had major fuel supplies at bases such as Diego Garcia or, alternatively, could buy oil from the littoral states. One of the least publicized changes in the American defense posture that has occurred since the Vietnam War concerns the oil factor. During the height of that war, U.S. forces used billions of gallons of oil for land, sea and air operations without seriously having to worry about the security or cost of supplies. A similar type of military operation in, say, the Persian Gulf area would now be much more constraining and disruptive of the U.S. domestic oil supply and prices.

On turning to the question of access to African resources, one finds conflicting views as to the strategic and long-term economic importance of Africa's mineral wealth. Nigerian and Cabindan oil is important but pales in comparison to the Persian Gulf supplies. There are alternative sources and in some cases substitutes for the many minerals such as gold, diamonds and the platinum groups found in South Africa. Furthermore, even if the mineral-producing countries were to fall into "hostile" hands, the chances are they would still *want* to sell their products to the West. On the other hand, hostile control of the minerals *could* lead to cut-offs, cut-backs, cartels, and, perhaps most significant, chaos on the money market. If South African gold production were to come under Soviet control, it would give the U.S.S.R. a virtual monopoly on the gold market, with possible difficulties for the stability of Western currencies. South Africa tends to cooperate about regulating its production rate to Western gold needs. There is no guarantee that a "hostile" power would be as forthcoming.

There is also the psychological importance of the economic wealth of South Africa and the setback if this were to fall into hostile hands. South Africa, after all, is the world's leading producer of vanadium, gold and platinum group metals, and antimony. It's the second largest producer of chrome (essential for the production of steel) and manganese ore. It contains 85 per cent of the world's reserve platinum and 80 per cent of the world's reserve chrome. South Africa also contains the second largest reserves of uranium in the Western world. In short, one cannot dismiss the importance of these minerals even if substitutes are available. They represent an economic asset which, in the complicated world of economic and strategic relations, have political significance beyond the strictly financial. Furthermore secure access to Africa's minerals requires the continuation of an effective mining and logistical infrastructure to extract and distribute minerals to distant markets. Civil disorder can disrupt the mineral flow as well as more overt military and political control can.

POSSIBLE THREATS TO U.S. STRATEGIC INTERESTS

In examining the various threats to U.S. strategic interests, it should be said at the outset that a wide range can be anticipated and analyzed. They extend from "low-level" threats posed by "neutral" black regimes unwilling to provide the U.S. Navy with bunkering facilities to "high-level" threats such as a Soviet naval presence in a "liberated" South Africa, the Horn of Africa and West Africa. In order to demonstrate the range of activities that can be anticipated, and their relative seriousness for the West and the United States, four categories of threats will be examined: first, threats posed by hostile black regimes in a situation where the current regime in South Africa remains in power; second, threats posed by a neutral, potentially hostile, black South Africa; third, threats posed by a Soviet maritime presence in black Africa but excluding South Africa; and fourth, threats posed by a Soviet presence in a "liberated" South Africa.

Within these four categories of threats, two types of hostile action will be considered: first, indirect or negative threats to Western interests, such as the denial of access to facilities and minerals; and second, direct, more positive threats, including the use of force to threaten or attack Western military forces and commerce.

Two types of general conditions will be examined: first, a "peacetime" crisis situation where the United States needs to deploy forces into the Indian Ocean-South Atlantic region; and second, a wartime situation which envisages a major worldwide conflict between the NATO and the Warsaw Pact forces.

Threat No. 1: Black States Neutral—South Africa Still Pro-West

This is the situation the United States generally faces today. The effects of a denial of black African facilities would be more of a nuisance than anything else, slowing down U.S. reaction time during a crisis in the Indian Ocean. Ironically, it can be argued that these constraints would be less troublesome in wartime or in serious crisis since it can be assumed that

South Africa would make its facilities available and the United States would have far less compunction about using them in these circumstances.

In the event that the black countries were prepared to engage in hostile actions against U.S. surface vessels, they might pose some marginal threat to a stray American or European warship in the region, given their current levels of arms. As yet, they have no real military ability to threaten Western forces in the region; but in view of the rate at which many of the black African countries are arming and given new technologies for anti-shipping missiles, a future situation might arise whereby some of the African countries could raise the military costs to the West of access to certain sea areas (e.g., the Mozambique Channel or the Guinea Basin).

In a wartime situation, again ironically, the military threats of black African countries would be less troublesome since, if they were to engage in hostilities toward Western shipping, retaliatory measures would be taken and, in any foreseeable military exchange, the Western powers have more than enough capacity to neutralize the embryonic maritime forces of the black African states.

In terms of minerals, there is little evidence that under the present conditions even the more "hostile" black African states will forfeit the economic benefits of selling minerals to the West. Hence the Angola regime has continued to maintain close relations with American companies, especially Gulf Oil, despite Western support for its foes. However, as has been pointed out, a willingness to sell minerals may not be enough, especially if civil and military strife is present within the mineral-producing country. The MPLA regime in Angola has not been able to keep the critical Benguela railway open for the past two years. This has not only disrupted the Angolan economy but has caused Zaire to export its copper via

Rhodesia and South Africa. In a wartime situation, South Africa would presumably still provide its resources to the West.

Threat No. 2: South Africa Neutral, Potentially Hostile

In this situation, it is assumed that a government has come to power in South Africa which, in all probability, is black, neutral if not hostile toward Western strategic interests, but has not provided military facilities to the Soviet Union. The denial of South African facilities in the peacetime crisis would have more a psychological than a military effect since the United States does not use very many of these facilities now except for intelligence gathering. (The absence of the intelligence gathering would be a problem but not an insurmountable one. It should be remembered that until very recently the United States had difficulty communicating with U.S. ships as they moved around the Cape. This now has been overcome by much more sophisticated satellite communications. Some, but certainly not all, intelligence information, for instance on ship movements, could also come from satellites.)

In a wartime situation, a neutral or hostile South Africa could pose difficulties to the West even without a Soviet presence. The South African government presumably would have at its disposal more sophisticated maritime forces than other black African countries have and would, therefore, be able to pose, in theory, a more immediate threat to Western shipping in that region. It should be remembered that the current South African regime has built up one of the most sophisticated maritime forces in the less-industrial world, which includes submarines, destroyers, maritime reconnaissance aircraft, and fast-patrol boats.[4] However, to offset this, it

[134]

can be argued that unless a black regime employed the skilled white population to run its armed forces, the effectiveness of the sophisticated hardware and infrastructure would be severely constrained for a long period of time, thereby diminishing its military utility.

In regard to mineral access, a hostile South African government could create very serious problems for the Western economies, especially in a crisis situation. By withholding gold or alternatively flooding the market with gold, the delicate mechanisms of Western finance *might* be seriously jeopardized. Although this threat falls more under the category of "economic warfare," it is not one that can be easily brushed aside. Denial of such other South African minerals as chrome and uranium would have both economic and military implications, though in the latter case much would depend upon the extent of Western stockpiles.

Threat No. 3: Soviet Military Presence in Black Africa—South Africa Pro-West

Before assessing the Soviet threat, a word should be said about Soviet intentions and capabilities in the region. Soviet strategic interests, like Western interests, in the southern seas cannot be decoupled from broader political and economic factors. There are a number of theses as to why the Soviet Union should wish to pursue a forward policy in the area. They include arguments to the effect that, in terms of its long-range global strategy, the Soviet Union sees Africa as a way of eventually penetrating South America and thereby isolating its major adversary, the United States, from its traditional friends and allies. At the other extreme, some see the Soviet presence as primarily opportunistic, with no clearly thought-out blue-

[135]

print for regional hegemony (see Chapter 5). Others would argue the importance of Sino-Soviet competition in Africa, while some see the Soviet presence in economic terms. The Soviet Union needs the fish of the South Atlantic and, having been forbidden to fish off the coast of Latin America and increasingly denied fishing rights in the North Atlantic, it is wooing African countries with aid in order to "buy in" to their rich fishing areas.

From a strictly military perspective, the Soviet Union can be said to have several interests; first, to be able to pose some threat to the NATO SLOCs across the North Atlantic. Michael MccGwire has argued that the Soviet Union has "shown a consistent interest in the latitude band 10°N-20°N, which takes in the bulge of West Africa, the Cape Verde Islands, and the southern half of the Caribbean." If the Soviet Union were to establish a more serious maritime presence in this region, it would have excellent surveillance access and could pose some threat to the NATO fleets. MccGwire has also argued that the Soviet Union regards the Cape route as a potentially important SLOC for supporting its Far Eastern commitments, for the Soviet Union, like the West, could easily be denied access through Suez in a crisis of war. Furthermore, it can only use its northern sea route to the Far East for about one-third of the year.[5]

There is also the more contentious issue of possible Soviet designs on the West's access to Middle East oil. Persian Gulf oil supplies are vulnerable to direct Soviet military action at three points in the flow-cycle: at the source, in transit, and at the terminals in Europe, Japan and North America. Most of the oil extraction facilities of the Middle East are land based; most of the oil is delivered to Europe and Japan by sea.

Threats to the extraction facilities are confined to the Persian Gulf region. In the event of a decision to attack the oil supplies in transit, Soviet maritime forces in the Indian Ocean and South Atlantic have two basic military options: they can try to blockade or mine narrow choke-points such as Hormuz and Bab-el-Mandeb, or they can sink oil tankers along the SLOC. Given the *current* disposition of Soviet and Western maritime forces in the southern seas, the threat by submarine, surface ship and land-based air is not very credible, although this could change if a Soviet build-up were to continue to be unchecked by the West; and if the Soviet Union were ever to establish major military bases in sub-Saharan Africa, the threat from all three components would be much greater.[6]

Although a good deal has been written on the importance of the Cape route and the supposed correlation between the growing importance of the oil traffic and the emergence of a Soviet maritime presence in the region, there is little evidence that at present the Soviet Union has any intention, let alone capability, of interfering with oil supplies transported *around the Cape,* although as will be pointed out later, this could change over time.

In the event of a crisis in the Middle East-Persian Gulf region in which the West wished to deploy forces from the Atlantic into the Indian Ocean and could not use Suez, a Soviet military presence in black Africa would cause concern but would probably be manageable. The Soviet Union would be unlikely to have the military capabilities of the Western navies in this region and would therefore, most probably, use its navies more to register a political presence.[7]

In the event of war, the Soviet presence in black Africa would, of course, be more serious. But if we assume a pro-West South Africa, the Soviet Union would have to count on South African participation with the Western forces, and South Africa would therefore be used as a base from which to threaten the Soviet facilities. Since their facilities would probably not be as good as those available to the West, an engagement might cause more military problems for the Soviet Union than for the West. However, to offset this, it must be emphasized that the West has far greater commercial stakes in the region than the Soviet Union has and, therefore, more to lose in the event of war.

Threat No. 4: Soviet Military Presence in South Africa, the Horn, and West Africa

This option would probably be of the most concern to U.S. and Western military planners (being, in fact, a "worse case" analysis). Since South Africa's facilities are excellent, with major bases in South Africa the Soviet Union would be able effectively to control the Cape. Its maritime air, submarine force and surface fleet and its control of communications would pose major risks for any Western naval or commercial vessels in the entire southern seas region. This does not mean, of course, that the West would be excluded from the southern seas since there are fall-back positions, including islands owned by Britain and France, such as Ascension, St. Helena, and Reunion. But an active Soviet military presence would, by all accounts, represent a dramatic change in the balance of power in this region.

In a peacetime crisis situation, the United States could probably still operate in areas such as the Arabian Sea even if the Soviet Union controlled southern Africa and the Horn since there are alternative routes and Western military strength is still considerable. But the psychological importance of the Soviet presence might well persuade the United States and other Western powers to hesitate before committing

[138]

themselves in a major way to potential conflict in this region. Furthermore, the effects upon the perceptions of countries in the Middle East and South America would be especially profound.

A wartime scenario with the Soviet Union in effective control of facilities in sub-Saharan Africa would be extremely serious, depending upon the anticipated timeframe of the war. A short war in Europe in which one side won or a ceasefire was reached would obviously have a less serious effect upon Persian Gulf oil supplies than a long war depending upon the level of stockpiles.[8] But in a protracted war of attrition in which nuclear weapons were not used for one reason or another, its control of this route would give the Soviet Union a great initial advantage. If the West were to attempt a direct strike on Soviet facilities in South Africa, the distances are great and a Western air attack against, say, Simonstown, would be difficult even with B-52s rotated out of Diego Garcia.

Over time, however, it is not clear that the Russians would be able to maintain a military foothold in South Africa in war since they themselves are extremely vulnerable at their own points of egress around the Soviet littoral. Thus, if the West were able to bottle up the Soviet Northern, Pacific, Mediterranean and Baltic fleets, residual Soviet naval forces in the southern seas would be isolated from the Soviet Union, and the Western control of the North Atlantic would pose a major threat to the Soviet control of the South Atlantic and Western Indian Ocean.

With respect to minerals, absolute Soviet control of Africa's resources, especially those of southern Africa, would obviously be of great significance in view of its own huge supplies of oil and uranium and the impact this would have on the Western demand for and access to these products. However, here one must distinguish between positive "control" in the sense of operational control of mineral extraction and distribution facilities and negative "control" which relates more to the ability to deny minerals to the West. In the first case the Soviet Union would be able to count Africa's mineral wealth alongside its own inventory in calculating the economic and strategic benefits of a policy of providing or denying minerals to Western markets. In the second case it could count upon the elimination or reduction of Africa's input into the world demand but could not actively manipulate African mineral production. Short of Soviet occupation of Africa, the second contingency seems more likely than the first.

In summarizing the external scenarios, there is only one contingency which would pose a potentially vital threat to the West, namely, a *major* Soviet maritime presence in the bulge of Africa, the Horn, and South Africa. The advent of black rule in South Africa and a limited Soviet presence in some of the black African countries would have more political implications than strategic ones. But since there are always linkages between psychological, political, and strategic factors, the events of the past two years (which include the use of Cubans) cannot be ignored, especially if they impinge upon the West's critical strategic interests in the Persian Gulf. For instance, if the Soviet Union's African policy helps it to undermine the Western presence and influence in the Gulf, the United States should develop contingencies against it. In military terms this means countering Soviet activities in the South Atlantic and Indian Ocean. In practice, this will probably entail a continued military presence in the Indian Ocean, with support provided by the island bases in the Indian Ocean and possibly in the South Atlantic.

[140]

Arms Sales

In examining all these contingencies we have been considering their possible impact—not their likelihood of occurring. When considering the relationship between African real estate and conflicts occurring on the high seas or in distant regions in the Indian Ocean, it should be emphasized that the likelihood of an increased Soviet military presence in Africa is not unrelated to the domestic events in sub-Saharan Africa itself. The complex problems of internal African conflict cannot be ignored. For the United States two issues raised by internal African crises—and possible Soviet participation therein—are particularly important: military aid and arms sales to the sub-Saharan African countries, and pressures for U.S. military intervention there.

With regard to arms sales there are no easy answers. However, several factors, not the least of them Soviet arms policy, indicate that U.S. arms transfers to Africa have become an important issue in the context of both the U.S. domestic debate on arms sales and the pursuit of U.S. strategic interests. Most African countries are engaged in fairly expensive programs of military modernization. Several of them at present face serious military threats from neighbors. Thus the demand for arms in Africa is both real and growing. U.S. arms and training can be used to cultivate and support moderate, pro-Western black African regimes which face threats from neighboring hostile, anti-Western states. U.S. arms sales to Kenya would presumably fall into this category. In the future, the United States might well want to consider similar transfers to Zambia, and possibly to Zimbabwe (Rhodesia) if and when a moderate black regime assumes office after the resignation or ouster of the Smith regime. Such a policy would call for the transfer of small amounts of fairly basic military equipment, training and infrastructure, as distinct from the enormous amounts of equipment provided to Middle Eastern countries.

The advantages of such a policy are several, including political influence and greater military stability for a friendly regime. More negatively, it can be argued that if the United States turns down requests from such countries, it can hardly expect to reap the benefits of close amicable cooperation with them in dealings on other factors that influence U.S. interests.

This type of classic dilemma is well illustrated by U.S. arms sales to Zaire, at present facing a military insurgency in the south as the Angolan-backed Katangan guerrillas challenge Zaire's sovereignty of Shaba province. The case for providing arms to Zaire is strong. Zaire, after all, is a pro-Western mineral-rich country; Angola is radical and is supported by the Soviet Union and Cuba. In the context of U.S. policy toward Africa, however, military sales to Zaire represent a deliberate attempt to "compete" with the Soviet Union and set precedents that may not be desirable for other areas such as the Horn.

In consequence, the major disadvantages or costs of increased U.S. arms sales to Africa deserve a careful hearing. By transferring arms we invariably contribute to the greater militarization of the continent. Black African countries have scarce resources, and to divert money and skilled manpower to weapons is not, in the long run, going to assure their stability. Few, if any, of the "moderate" black regimes are democratic by Western standards; and therefore the human rights issue, which has bedevilled our arms-transfer relationships with Latin America, could surface in Africa. (How could we justify selling arms to Zaire or Somalia while not permitting Ecuador to buy Israeli jets?) Another cost would be the possible involve-

[142]

ment of the United States in commitments which, in turn, might increase the probabilities and pressures for U.S. intervention if a serious military conflict were to erupt.[9] This could be particularly serious in the case of the Rhodesian conflict.

As for possible arms sales to South Africa—assuming there is no possibility of any sales to Rhodesia—there are two sets of circumstances when such sales should at least be considered in the context of strategic interests. The first would be a situation in which South Africa was actively under siege and the Soviet Union was involved in the fighting. In this case, U.S. transfers could be contemplated on the following grounds: they might reduce pressure from some circles for the United States to intervene to protect the white population of South Africa; they might strengthen the ability of the South African armed forces to withstand attacks, thereby embroiling the Soviet Union in a quagmire; they might be necessary to stave off a Soviet victory which would result in the capture or control of the Cape province.

The arguments against arms transfers to the white government of South Africa are more persuasive and more likely in any case to prevail. The main argument against such sales is based upon domestic, political realities of the United States. So long as the black constituency in the United States has influence over the administration, an effective veto will almost certainly ensue on arms sales to the white regime. The only circumstances under which this could change would be in a dire emergency when the President was able to argue that U.S. strategic objectives should override political and ideological arguments.

Finally, there is the question of U.S. arms supplies to non-state actors, especially guerrilla organizations. Here the problems are equally complex. There is considerable support in certain U.S. political groups for the objectives of the black "liberation" movements committed to the violent overthrow of the white regimes in Rhodesia and South Africa. Arms aid to guerrillas might provide the United States with useful counter-leverage against the U.S.S.R., which is at present the major arms supplier. This, in turn, might help to influence the types of governments which came to power in Rhodesia, and possibly even South Africa. The arguments against such sales, however, are likely to prevail for, in much the same way that the black and liberal constituency in the United States has an effective veto. on U.S. sales to South Africa, so there will almost certainly be a strong constituency in the United States opposing all sales to radical guerrilla groups committed to the violent overthrow of legally constituted regimes such as that in South Africa.

In sum, on all issues pertaining to U.S. arms sales to Africa, there is great scope for controversy and profound disagreement as to the wisdom of such activities. Although the amounts of arms will never approach those of other major areas such as the Middle East and Europe, the political importance of the issue far outweighs the dollar values involved. Invariably when faced with these sorts of trade-offs, decision-makers revert to the age-old practice of "case-by-case analysis." This means that no blueprints for determining preferred arms-transfer policies to black African countries will, in fact, ever be used. Instead, the approval or denial of sales to, say, Zimbabwe, would be judged in the broader context of the southern African political and strategic environment. Such a policy approach certainly has merit in contrast to the utterances of those who believe the United States should not sell instruments of war to most Third World countries. Fortunately there seems to be a growing awareness in the Carter administration that the costs and benefits of denying or supplying military aid to African countries are complicated, to say the least.

U.S. Intervention in Southern Africa

With all the uncertainty concerning future events in sub-Saharan Africa, most seasoned observers feel confident of one prediction, namely, that conflict and violence will continue. So long as these occur, the possibilities for U.S. intervention have to be considered.

In the case of Rhodesia, there seems little prospect that the United States would ever even consider intervening militarily, were the situation to deteriorate. (It is conceivable that U.S. troops might be sent in as part of a "peace-keeping" force in order to protect lives or to help evacuate the white population if radical blacks eventually take power.) However, if a change of government in Rhodesia comes about through bloodshed rather than negotiation, it will be a signal to the South African population that a future war in the south is probably inevitable. It is at this juncture that the dilemmas would begin to mount, for now the United States would have to treat seriously the possibility of a protracted military conflict in South Africa, which, over time, could run the risks of involving the military forces of the Soviet Union and, therefore, possibly those of the United States.

In any analysis of South Africa, one invariably has to face up to the prospects for conflict and the role that force would play in that conflict. This derives from the intractable nature of the problem. South Africa is so different from Rhodesia, Mozambique, or Angola that comparisons are not only meaningless but misleading. The concept of eventual "majority rule" in

South Africa without any reference to a territorial settlement between the various races is analogous to the concept of "majority rule" in Palestine. (And, indeed, if the Palestine analogy has any relevance at all, it would be that eventual partition of South Africa may be the only long-term avenue for negotiations.)**

One thing seems likely: the more protracted a conflict in South Africa, the more difficult for the United States to remain indifferent. It is not the purpose of this essay to speculate about how such a major conflict in South Africa could come about. In the event that it did though, there are two usual scenarios: one posits an external threat either landward or seaward, or both; the other posits an internal threat in the form of rebellion and urban insurgency. There is also the possibility of simultaneous internal and external conflict.

"The prospects for a direct invasion or blockade of South Africa are militarily unrealistic and are likely to remain so for years to come. South Africa has by far the most effective military forces in sub-Saharan Africa, including those of Nigeria. The South Africans have an indigenous armaments industry and are technically capable, given the terrain and geography, of sustaining a fairly protracted war. They have stockpiled at least a two-year's supply of oil. The white, Afrikaans-speaking majority seems likely to continue determined to fight rather than surrender. Since whites control most of the strategic assets, any violent conflict would probably be bloody and the outcome far from clear. Thus there is a possibility that were the Soviet Union or the black African countries to embark on a war against white South Africa they might well find themselves engaged in a long war. In this case one might ask to what extent U.S. interests would

[146]

be served by joining the attack, adopting strict neutrality, or, alternatively, providing covert help to the whites.

One variation on the first option would be for the United States to forestall the Soviet Union and other Communist countries by helping the radical blacks in the "crusade" at the very beginning of a conflict. By assisting the forces of "progress" the United States would assure a friendly regime in South Africa and would, *en passant,* deny the Soviet Union the prospects of the political, economic, and possibly military fruits of victory. However, direct U.S. support for black states and guerrilla groups would meet major resistance within the United States and Western Europe and would, therefore, probably be ruled out by any administration. Equally, if not more so, support for a white regime against a black coalition of forces would have serious domestic costs. (The West Europeans might be able to help South Africa since they have more at stake economically, but they, too, would find domestic opposition to such activity.)

The option that seems most viable for the United States would be strict *military* neutrality. The rationale for neutrality would be based on the hope that a peaceful solution to such a conflict could be found and, alternatively, that if military conflict continued, the white South Africans would be sufficiently strong to deny the Soviet Union a major victory but *not* strong enough to prevent drastic political and economic reform and social change in that country.

It can be safely predicted that none of these options will be so simple. Inevitably, events will occur that were not anticipated; the white South Africans might crumble more quickly than imagined. The greatest weaknesses and, therefore, vulnerability of the white regime are its dependence upon black labor to sustain its industrial productivity and its

[147]

psychological fear of black violence. To this extent the most critical strategic factor *within* South Africa would be the relative strength of the urban blacks and the ability of the regime to control that group in the event of insurrection. Based upon the experiences of other industrial countries and given the unique physical separation of the black urban areas from the center of power, it can be argued that such an insurrection could be fairly easily, if somewhat bloodily, contained. The most decisive weapon of the black population is economic; and a coordinated effort to withhold labor, in parallel to the sporadic use of violence, would be extremely threatening to the regime.

If South Africa were threatened externally, the white regime might take the offensive and carry a war to the north, threatening black, Russian, and Cuban military expeditionary forces in the region. In such circumstances, the embryonic South African nuclear weapons program must be taken at face value and, over the years, could become an issue in the strategic equation.

Elsewhere in sub-Saharan Africa the likelihood of U.S. strategic interests being served by unilateral *direct* intervention is remote. In most contingencies, e.g., chaos in Zaire or Kenya following a succession crisis, the only justification for the use of U.S. forces—aside from humanitarian "rescue" missions— would be to check a direct Soviet intervention with ground troops. While this is possible, it, too, has a low probability unless it is part of an overall East-West crisis involving other strategic theaters such as the Middle East. This does not mean the United States would have to avoid all embroilments in black African crises. The role of covert operations, while frowned upon by the U.S. administration and public at present, may become more acceptable as a policy option in the future. It is not difficult to think of future contingencies where

[148]

well-planned covert operations could effectively serve U.S. interests. The mistakes of the recent past should not be allowed to proscribe indefinitely the use of such methods if the national interest warrants it.

In pursuing policies which will contribute to its overall foreign policy objectives, the United States faces hard choices in several areas. While there probably will be little dispute that a major Soviet military presence in sub-Saharan Africa would pose a strategic threat to the West, there will be much less consensus as to whether, in fact, the Soviet Union is actively pursuing this objective, what success it may have, and, beyond this, what the preferred U.S. responses should be. At one extreme, there are those who argue that the Soviet threat is minimal, that it is primarily reactive, that the critical U.S. interests are not strategic but political and moral, that arms sales rarely serve political interests. Therefore, they conclude, the preferred policy for the United States should be to adopt an active "pro-black," "pro-human rights" policy toward sub-Saharan Africa and avoid the temptation to be drawn into providing either covert support to South Africa or arms supplies to black governments. Instead, economic and diplomatic aid should be stressed.

At the other extreme, there are those who see the Soviet threat as growing and who go so far as to equate each Soviet fishing vessel in the South Atlantic as a potential threat to U.S. warships and Western oil tankers. This school would support strong measures to check Soviet activity, including covert operations against Cuban- and Soviet-backed regimes, a build-up of U.S. naval power in the South Atlantic and Indian Ocean, and implicit support for South Africa.

In between the two extreme positions lies a whole range of practical approaches. The most reasonable variant, it seems to

[149]

me, is the argument that although the Soviet threat is potentially real enough, it can, and has been, exaggerated. As far as the Soviet-Cuban presence in Angola and Ethiopia is concerned, the United States should wait and see how deeply embroiled the Communist countries really are before taking more active and escalatory steps to challenge them. If indeed they appear to be moving into a quagmire, this may serve our interests, provided they do not overreact by escalating their own involvement. If, however, their involvement appears to give a decisive military victory to their clients, the implications would be sufficiently serious to require a strong Western response, if necessary with military aid and a direct presence but also involving covert operations.

In the broader geopolitical context of the southern seas, appropriate military policies for the United States are more clear-cut. In order to balance and deter the Soviet Union, low-keyed U.S. initiatives to maintain a military footing in the South Atlantic and the Indian Ocean should be continued. This would involve continued support for the Diego Garcia base, irrespective of the so-called Zone of Peace proposals which call for a mutual termination of U.S. and Soviet base rights in the Indian Ocean. It would also support continued and perhaps increased deployments of U.S. carrier task forces into both the South Atlantic and Indian Oceans for periods of each year, which preferably would be coordinated with NATO forces, especially Britain's and France's. Such initatives would, in my opinion, be sufficient to protect vital Western strategic interests in the Persian Gulf area from Soviet-inspired threats from Africa.

NOTES

1. This thesis is outlined in Geoffrey Kemp, "The New Strategic Map," *Survival,* the Journal of the International Institute for Strategic Studies, March/April 1977.

2. This section on the Cape Route draws upon material in "The South Atlantic as a Strategic Theater," prepared by the author for the Study Group on U.S. Interests in the South Atlantic, Institute for Foreign Policy Analysis, Cambridge, Mass., 1977.

3. The Cape route is also one of the world's most polluted areas. The pollution is primarily due to oil spills, both accidental and deliberate. The extent to which these oil spills may eventually jeopardize the balances within the ecological region and in the Antarctic area is not yet known, but this problem needs to be watched carefully since it is the type of issue which could give ammunition to *any* South African government should it wish to extend a pollution-control zone out to 100 or 200 miles, somewhat similar to the zone adopted by Canadians.

4. South Africa's maritime forces have been procured and deployed to meet two types of seaward threat; the conventional and the unconventional. The conventional seaward threat refers to the possibility of Soviet naval interference with the Cape route and the possibility of intervention or blockade by the great powers acting with or without the approval of the U.N. or OAU. The unconventional seaward threat relates to possible guerrilla infiltration by sea from the north along the long coastlines.

5. Michael MccGwire, "Soviet Interest and Capabilities in the South Atlantic Region: 1977-1990." Paper prepared for the Study Group on U.S. Interests in the South Atlantic, Institute for Foreign Policy Analysis, Cambridge, Mass., March 2, 1977. The most

[151]

serious threat to NATO would be if the Soviet Union could use these new facilities for refueling and resupplying its ships and aircraft, especially the submarines and *Backfire* bombers which at present operate out of the Kola peninsula and have to run the gauntlet of Western choke-points in the northern seas in order to get into and return from the Atlantic proper.

6. In the opinion of the author, by far the most serious Soviet *political-military* threat to Persian Gulf oil is in the Gulf itself. A future contingency whereby the Soviet Union might be "invited" in to protect a radical Arab government, possibly a future Saudi Arabian regime, would be especially divisive to the West since it would not necessarily involve a cut-off in oil supplies. It can be argued that the Soviet Union has infinitely more to gain from "controlling" oil suppliers rather than destroying the oil fields.

7. These capabilities could of course improve over time. If the Soviet Union had military facilities in Guinea, Angola, and possibly Namibia, as well as Somalia and the People's Democratic Republic of Yemen, it could patrol virtually the entire West African littoral and begin to pose some threat to South Africa itself, as well as threaten the Persian Gulf and U.S. reinforcements sent into the Indian Ocean for staging out of Diego Garcia.

8. For a thorough treatment of the oil stockpile question, see Edward N. Krapels, "Oil and Security Problems and Prospects of Importing Countries," *Adelphi Paper No. 136,* International Institute for Strategic Studies (London: Summer, 1977).

9. A possibly desirable alternative policy option would be to urge Europeans rather than the United States, to sell arms to black African countries. The Europeans, after all, have much closer links with many of them. They need the markets, and the arms, if they serve our interests at all, could probably just as well come from Italy or France or Britain as from the United States.

[152]

[FIVE]

The Soviet Union's Strategic Stake in Africa

Robert Legvold

Again Africa is challenging the indifference of most who know little about the area. For two reasons: One, developments in southern Africa (in Rhodesia, Namibia, and ultimately South Africa itself, and in the so-called Horn of Africa—the tinderbox containing Ethiopia and Somalia) have and will again menace the tranquility of international relations far beyond these immediate regions. Second, the Soviet Union and the United States are once more turning the region into an important area of competition, a competition which both see as strategic—in the double sense of deciding (1) who will exert greater influence over the course of change in Africa, and (2) who will dominate the ocean-ways to the east and the west. Both the potential crises and the competition are intertwined: The competition risks contaminating the crises and accentuating their impact outside the continent; the potential crises intensify the competition and give it a crude or primitive

[153]

quality. But any competition that assumes a largely political-military character tends to be crude or primitive, and this time around we and they are making the military dimension central.

Lamentable as it may be from the perspective of those who understand this continent and believe the focus of policy should be less superficial, Africa's crises and the Soviet-American competition will almost certainly determine the amount and kind of attention we give the area in the next several years. So both deserve careful study. Each is an essential point of departure in assessing the Soviet Union's military involvement in Africa. And I will make them together the core of these comments.

The first half of my essay deals with basic aspects of the Soviet-American competition—the Soviet stake in the area and the role it assigns military power. Treated first, this gives a better basis for judging the part the Soviet Union may or may not play should matters boil over in Rhodesia or should the violence in the Horn erupt in renewed war. Thus, initially, I will look at the link Soviet analysts draw between military power and their country's African policy, then at their view of the direction of trends in Africa, and eventually at the stake they apparently feel their country has so far from home. The point of reviewing these basic considerations, however, is to provide a more suitable perspective from which to assess the Soviet Union's specific military activity in this area and to understand the role that the Soviet Union has reserved for itself in Africa's troubled regions.

I. THE SOVIET CONCEPTION OF MILITARY POWER IN THIRD WORLD REGIONS

Two things stand out: *First,* in Soviet military theory, doctrine, and strategy, there is no direct guidance for the use of military force in outlying areas like Africa. Soviet thought is, or was until recently, designed for Europe and for nuclear war with the United States. The distraction introduced by China has divided the Soviet Union's attention and forced a partial adjustment of doctrine but no fundamental revision of theory and certainly no invention of theory to cover the use of military force in Third World conflicts.

Thus, despite all its emphasis on wars of national liberation, the Soviet Union has had no particular notion of how to fight them and no particular inclination to incorporate them into its overall military posture or its basic theory of deterrence. Nearly twenty years ago the United States devised the notion of "flexible response" or graduated deterrence, in part, in order to deal with violence and conflict in secondary areas. But the Soviet Union has never developed an equivalent concept. Instead, it has persisted with a rudimentary notion of deterrence roughly similar to the original American theory of "massive retaliation" and a military strategy premised on massed and highly mobile conventional forces poised to wage a rapid, short *blitzkrieg* war in Europe. (Though of fundamental importance in most other contexts, there is no need here to linger over the fact that the Soviet Union apparently embraces none of our notions of deterrence—neither those related to "minimum deterrence" nor those emphasizing restraint in use—or the fact that it lives with "mutual assured destruction," not out of choice, but momentarily for want of a choice.)

Yet, on the other hand, over the last several years the Soviet

[155]

Union has considerably increased its ability to project military power far from the continent of Eurasia. This gives special meaning to the *second* fact conspicuous in Soviet analysis, i.e., a keen sensitivity to the political significance and utility of military force. Here an important distinction needs to be drawn between (1) the instrumentalism of war (which is not demonstrable in Soviet analysis) and (2) the instrumentalism of military power (which is). Soviet theory does not treat war as such as a legitimate instrument of policy, except wars of liberation fought by the colonially oppressed who have no alternative. (Their attachment to Clausewitz's dictum that "war is an extension of policy" leads to much misunderstanding on this score.) But Soviet theory does recognize a direct relationship between foreign policy and military power.

Soviet analysts have long contended that military force is not only an important element among the West's policy resources but the central one. This is where they start. The United States' military power, they say, is not merely the outcome of interest-group competition within the American defense establishment, any more than it is the innocent by-product of the interaction between Soviet and American defense efforts. It is, according to them, a consciously and carefully composed auxiliary of policy. We have built a range of military force with the needs of policy in mind.

The interesting thing is that they do not repudiate this relationship. Unlike the utility which they say we see in war, a value which they reject, they do not deny in principle the virtue of tailoring military power to foreign policy—only the way we do the tailoring. On the contrary, Soviet specialists now write openly about the need to devise ways of "combining" military power "with other policy means" and finding "proper solutions" for the "serious military policy problems that will arise."

[156]

Several considerations follow from this last point. First, because Soviet analysts have traditionally regarded our ability to intervene militarily as a key aspect of our effort to influence, even control, change in the Third World—indeed, to listen to them, this is the one instance in which the *political* significance of military power is demonstrable—they can be expected to seek much the same. At a minimum they would like to have the means to prevent us from intervening at will, and we would be foolish to assume that they intend to stop short of acquiring it. There is, of course, a fundamental difference between the kind of long-range sea and airlift capacity or the ability to project power needed to neutralize the other side's power to intervene and the resources needed to intervene freely yourself without fear of counteraction. This first has to do with *protecting* change supported by you and this seems to me to be a long-term Soviet objective. The other has to do with *forcing* change, and that cannot be either proved or disproved as a Soviet objective. (Just as there is no proving or disproving the Soviet desire for military superiority over the United States. Rather, the relevant questions are (1) whether the Soviet Union thinks it already has superiority; (2) if not, whether it thinks it could have superiority; and (3), if so, how much it is willing to sacrifice in pursuing superiority.) These are the prior questions and so is the essential question of protecting rather than forcing change.

Second, the Soviet Union has over the last decade substantially enhanced its ability to project military power. True, these efforts still command but a small portion of Soviet defense resources, at that, a relatively constant portion. And, true, the Soviet ability to project power is but a shadow of our own: It has no floating air bases comparable to our thirteen carriers, a naval infantry that is less than a tenth of the U.S. Marine corps, one-fifth the amphibious force, a fraction of our airlift capacity, a vastly inferior "underway replenishment capability," and only the most rudimentary infrastructure of foreign "bases."

Yet, while these discrepancies help to keep matters in perspective, there is no gainsaying the emergence of a real Soviet ability to project military power to areas where earlier this was simply missing. Contrast the 85,000 tons of equipment delivered to the Arabs by sea on 30 freighters during the 1973 war and the additional 15,000 ferried in on more than 1,000 flights of AN-22 and AN-12 transport aircraft with Khrushchev's empty rhetorical flourishes in 1956. Or, more to the point, contrast the $200 million in military assistance brought to Angola over the critical months of 1975 by sea and air (46 flights of Soviet medium and heavy air transports alone), not to mention the airlift on Soviet IL-62s of a sizable part of the 11,000 Cuban troops sent during this period, with the paltry offering of a few trucks and 16 transport planes provided Lumumba in 1960. In any future African military conflict the Soviet Union will represent a potentially critical patron, able to supply in quantity a wide array of armaments and to get them to an area with dispatch.

Moreover, the Soviet Union is now constructing components that are expressly part of a force useable in distant places. For example, it has introduced a support ship, the *Boris Chilikin,* displacing 20,000 tons, and which is, according to *Jane's Fighting Ships,* the first genuine underway fleet replenishment ship built by the Soviet Navy. It is also hard at work on an enlarged heavy transport air capability, the core of which is the new IL-76 CANDID, a turbofan heavy freight-carrying transport aircraft roughly in a class with the American C-5A. These and other new items serve a variety of *wartime* purposes but, of interest here, they also provide the first traces of impatience with the Soviet Union's previous makeshift ability to project power. (Admittedly, the Soviet Union's ambition will not be indisputable until it begins to build amphibious assault forces large enough to operate beyond the immediate fleet areas and the tactical air necessary to cover operations. This it has not begun to do. This also, incidentally, is basically the minimum capability required if a nation believes in military power to *force* change.)

In the same way, the Soviet Union's apparent eagerness to secure the use of an ever larger number of facilities wherever the remotest possibility exists—from Portugal to Mozambique—adds further evidence that it intends to have military power readily at hand in areas like Africa. If there is any internal logic in the Soviet effort to accumulate a network of anchorages, bunkering facilities, airfields, communications, housing, and storage facilities in the Mediterranean and around the littoral of the Indian Ocean, it is to begin forming the infrastructure of a permanent military presence in these areas. Again, there are various reasons for wanting such facilities, not the least—indeed, above all—to counter American strategic (nuclear) naval forces and to offset our mastery of the seas. But surely the Soviet leadership also covets them for the power they permit the Soviet Union to bring to bear in any local conflict.

The third piece in this picture is a redefinition of the Soviet Navy's role to include far-reaching peacetime (political) tasks. Though perhaps as much exhortation as fixed policy, Admiral Gorshkov, the commander of the Soviet Navy, makes much of the distinction between these and basic war-related tasks. Some—such as the protection of "state interests"—we shall return to later, but two are worth noting in this context. One involves "increasing the Soviet Union's prestige and influence," by which he means the use of the naval arm to augment Soviet diplomacy—showing the flag, aiding with port-clearing operations, dispatching a cruiser or a pair of destroyers to places like Sierra Leone and Somalia when the position of the local leadership could use bolstering. The other he labels "countering imperialist aggression," and is a direct expression of the link between military power and foreign policy. Even more specifically, it is an excellent illustration of military power to "protect change." Thus, Gorshkov makes plain that the new forward-deployed Soviet Navy has a role to play in defending the "national liberation movement," a phrase representing whatever the Soviet Union regards as positive change in areas like Africa. To perform this task, he stresses (though whether as lobbyist or spokesman we do not know), the Soviet Navy must establish a (permanent) "presence" in these regions and on a scale grand enough to avoid "empty bluffing." So the circle is closed: From the fundamental proposition of military power's political utility to force planning to the elaboration of mission.

African Trends Through Soviet Eyes

Africa has been a harsh school for those who, like the Soviet Union (and the United States), arrived with preconceived notions of where events were moving. Beginning with Daniel Solod's expulsion from Guinea in November 1961 through the collapse of "revolutionary democratic" regimes in Ghana and Mali, to use the Soviet Union's once sanguine phrase, experience has taught the Soviet Union how much African societies are their own inspiration, how powerful traditional ways remain, and how great are the obstacles to a simple adaptation of "scientific socialism." Over the last decade and a half, the Soviet Union has learned to respect the limitations of Africa's most revolutionary leaderships and the frailty of the

[160]

revolutions they proclaim. It no longer has any illusions about the ease with which socialism will be constructed in places like Guinea or Congo-Brazzaville, let alone Mozambique, or about the setbacks that may follow, or about the compromises and retreats that may be necessary. And it certainly does not misunderstand the limits of its ability to command change, loyalty, deference, or favors from Africa's "progressive" regimes.

But not so long ago the Soviet Union was visibly discouraged by the basic rhythm of change in black Africa and now it no longer is. Soviet confidence in the underlying momentum of trends has been rejuvenated. Indeed, it now treats this area as politically one of the most dynamic in the global setting. The Soviet Union is not ignoring the dead hand of economic underdevelopment, but, from the perspective of politics, it finds more encouragement here than in virtually any other part of the Third World. This derives both from the transformations underway within a growing number of African countries and from the dramatic changes taking place in southern Africa. And both are, in the Soviet mind, mutually reinforcing.

For us in the West who tend to see no particular rapport between domestic trends within African countries and foreign policy imperatives (or opportunities)—perhaps because we, with reason, tend not to see patterns among these trends—the importance this perception has for the Soviet Union usually slips by us. Yet, the Soviet leaders do care about the balance of forces favoring or retarding the reorientation of African political systems and economies, and their mood depends to a considerable extent on their judgment of the state of this balance.

Thus, at the moment, they are feeling optimistic, and the reason has much to do with the prospect of some form of socialism catching on among an ever expanding number of African states. Ten years ago nothing of the kind existed. On the contrary, after the coup in Ghana in February 1966 and then Keita's overthrow two years later, Soviet analysts went into a bit of a funk. They drew back from Khrushchev's foolish formulas welcoming regimes like Nkrumah's, Keita's, or, for that matter, Ngouabi's into socialism, expunged from their commentary all traces of complacency, and concentrated on the mistakes made by Africa's leading "revolutionary democrats." Today, with the Soviet mood shifting, this is confessed: As one of their leading journalists recently wrote, in the face of these setbacks, the continued domination of "imperialist monopolies" almost everywhere, and the seemingly permanent instability, "many wondered whether Africa would hold out, whether there might be a repetition of the sad story of Latin America."

Since about 1972, and with special vigor since 1974, however, Soviet assessments have swung around decidedly. The reasons, I think, are three: First, what they feared might be a "counter-revolutionary" wave in black Africa never developed. The rise of military regimes did not turn out to be a way station to the "Latin Americanization" of Africa. And, by 1972, a country like Ghana appeared to be done with the moderate, pro-Western experiment of the Ankrah-Busia years.

Second, and far more important, by 1972 the number of African regimes declaring themselves socialist—even Marxist-Leninist—gradually began to mount. In Guinea, Touré seemed again back on track; in Somalia the revolution was gathering momentum; in Congo-Brazzaville the language was still more radical; and in Malagasy and Benin new regimes were in place that promised much the same. Moreover, Soviet analysts trusted more the wisdom of the new generation of revolutionary leaders—or so they said. That is, they trusted them to avoid what they called the "Leftist excesses" of the Malians and the carelessness of the Ghanaians who underestimated the "strength of the so-called 'new bourgeoisie' and the moribund classes—the feudals and the patriarchal-tribal elite opposed to the socialist orientation." They began to take note of the measured and systematic nationalization programs of these countries, the growth in the state sector, the attention paid grass-roots organizational work, the priority given agricultural development, and so on.[1] Slowly their tone grew less skeptical and admonitory and more encouraging, even confident.

In this evolution 1974 marks a watershed because of the sudden convergence of far-reaching change in a number of African countries. 1974 is the year of the Ethiopian "revolution"; the year Benin proclaimed its goal socialism (a year later Malagasy would adopt its Charter of the Socialist Revolution); it is the year of the Soviet-Somali Treaty of Friendship and Cooperation; and the year of the Second Congress of the Congolese Workers' Party. Combined with continued progress in Guinea, Tanzania, and Somalia, these events apparently persuaded Soviet observers that the African revolution had gathered its second wind. Since then, Soviet commentary has exuded an excitement and interest not evident since Khrushchev's last years.

The third and more momentous set of developments originated not in Africa but in Europe, in Portugal, where the April revolution transformed circumstances in southern Africa overnight. The liberation of Mozambique and Angola deeply affected Soviet perceptions—not merely because the situation was now radically altered for the white redoubts in Rhodesia and South Africa nor merely because Soviet access to this area would now surely grow, but because, in the Soviet estimation,

[163]

the breakthrough in southern Africa would greatly reinforce the process of social and political transformation elsewhere to the north. In fact, for them, the demise of the Portuguese colonial empire possesses a double significance: First, by sealing the fate of Rhodesia and Namibia and, ultimately, of South Africa, the revolution in Angola and Mozambique has reversed the historic balance in Africa. For, according to Soviet analysis, South Africa is the key to "progressive" change in the rest of Africa, particularly in those neighboring states held in economic vassalage. With this breach in the solidity of southern Africa and someday soon the end of the South African regime, Soviet commentators say, the most powerful revolutionary impulses now radiate from the south. Second, and closely related, the Soviet Union apparently views Third World revolutions forged in armed struggle as more profound than others and, therefore, considers the transformation underway in Mozambique and Angola as more secure, thus, in the long run a more substantial model for other parts of Africa.

I am not for a moment suggesting that the Soviet Union has been carried away by simple-minded revolutionary exuberance. I am not suggesting that it has deceived itself into believing that Africa is about to undergo a radical revolutionary transformation. Or that it thinks the central force in Africa is now the so-called countries of a "socialist orientation." Even less am I suggesting that the Soviet Union has subordinated policy to the promotion of the socialist revolution throughout Africa or even in Africa's major states. And still less that it has some grand vision of dividing Africa with a band of revolutionary states from Luanda to Maputo, then pushing north to the Red Sea, eventually creating a commonwealth of anti-Western states ascendant over all of East Africa.

But the Soviet Union does take seriously the basic drift to

events. From its vantage point, the historic struggle still is at the heart of political change, and nowhere more than in inchoate environments like Africa. To the extent that trends there appear to form a reassuring pattern, especially when in other areas like the Middle East they do not, the area holds a special interest for the Soviet Union. In Africa's case this is not enough to make it a region of high priority for Soviet policy—intrinsically Africa is simply not of that importance. And certainly it is not enough to justify paying much of a price. The Soviet Union, for example, is conspicuously uneager to inherit as an additional ward an economically troubled country like Mozambique. Thus, not only does it counsel against impetuous revolutionary measures that can only compound the country's difficulties, but it also apparently hopes that the West will continue to lend a hand.

THE SOVIET STAKE

Provided that we do not overstate the case, however, the Soviet Union does have a special stake in change within Africa. This is a renewed stake, because only a few years ago Soviet despair over the apparent failures of Africa's "revolutionary democracies" had led it to downplay the prospect of significant change and to concentrate on relations with non-revolutionary but inherently important states like Nigeria, Zaire, and Haile Selassie's Ethiopia.

But this is not a stake over which the Soviet Union feels it has enormous control. By and large, as the Soviet leaders know, change in Africa unfolds at its own pace and in its own fashion. There is change that the Soviet Union would be delighted to abet and, at the margin, it doubtless sees a role for itself. This role, however, is essentially as benefactor not

[165]

instigator. The military power flowing into the area, to the degree that it relates to the Soviet stake in internal change within Africa, has a subordinate and highly constrained function. It is not there, I think, to manufacture change, not there as the principal agent of the Soviet Union's engagement in Africa, and not there to seize every target of opportunity. Nor is it there under any illusion about how perfect the circumstances must be before it can be used: If its use means tangling with the United States Navy then the Soviet Union is not interested; if it means long-term and messy military entanglements then, again, the Soviet Union is not interested; and, by all indications, if it means running against the preferences of most of Africa, it is not interested. The Soviet leadership fully appreciates its disadvantage if military power is made the primary means by which the superpowers go about influencing change. Their country's inferiority begins with the resources it has (or not) to give as military assistance and ends with the proposition, to borrow from Michael Mcc-Gwire, that "only the United States has a world-wide capability to project force ashore against substantial opposition and without some measure of local support."

The Soviet Union has another stake in internal change within Africa: namely, its external stake in Africa. Or, stated another way, the Soviet Union is interested in promoting the kind of change easing its access to facilities that aid in the pursuit of its military-strategic objectives beyond Africa. The two "stakes," of course, interact. Facilities sustain power that may serve to protect and, once in a while, promote internal change; and the right kind of change enhances Soviet access to facilities. Unfortunately, too often we reduce the Soviet Union's stake in Africa to the external and, to the degree that we recognize the interaction of internal and external stakes, subordinate the internal to the external. Then to make matters worse we render this external stake in distorted or one-dimensional terms.

The Soviet Union's external stake in Africa, however, is extremely complex, diverse, and multidimensional. For simplicity's sake, I have divided it into four dimensions: (1) defensive national concerns, (2) defensive strategic concerns, (3) offensive national concerns, and (4) offensive strategic concerns. This is not the place to explore these categories in depth, but they can be summarized, and the summary serves to remind us that there is more behind Soviet military involvement in Africa than any one set of concerns.

To begin these categories in what seems to me to be the order of their priority: The first category, *defensive national concerns,* revolves around the imperative of protecting (a) the Soviet fishing fleet and (b) the shipping routes, particularly the Indian Ocean route from Soviet Europe to Soviet Asia. Over the last ten years the Soviet fishing fleet has gradually inched down the west coast of Africa and up the east coast. Now the second largest fishing fleet in the world, it takes more than 20 percent of its catch from the Indian Ocean alone. The Indian Ocean trade route is the only significant alternative link between the Soviet Union's two halves, other than the Tran-Siberian railroad network. Something like 18 percent of Soviet merchant shipping is concentrated there, though not only on the southern route for, the Soviet Union, too, is a user of the Cape trade route and it, too, is potentially vulnerable should the Suez Canal again be closed. Protecting these interests and the Soviet Union's increasing oceanographic and space-related activities constitutes a key purpose of Soviet military power in the region. These are, in part, what Gorshkov means by "state interests," and he lists protecting "state interests" as the first among the Soviet Navy's *peacetime* tasks.

Second, the Soviet Union has *defensive strategic concerns* in the area. These break down into: (a) coping with the American nuclear deterrent; (b) monitoring American, British, and French naval movements and, if need be, interposing Soviet naval power; (c) averting the expansion of American or Western bases/facilities in southern Africa, particularly, in South Africa and Namibia; and (d) disrupting any progress toward a NATO for the South Atlantic (a SATO), joining the military power of South Africa, Brazil, and Argentina, with or without the United States. The first of these, in fact, remains the highest priority of the Soviet Navy but, since the American deterrent depends only marginally on the Indian Ocean or the South Atlantic, I have ranked it lower here. Nonetheless the Soviet Union takes the task seriously enough to begin flying anti-submarine warfare (ASW) aircraft, such as they are, out of Angola. More important, the Soviet Union now has far better surveillance of the critical Central Atlantic because of the TU-95 BEAR patrols that it flies out of Conakry. Conakry completes a triangle (with the Northern Fleet airfields in the north and Cuban airfields in the west) making Soviet reconnaissance over this area far more comprehensive and flexible. Points (a) and (b) involve the acquisition of facilities. Points (c) and (d), however, depend directly and almost wholly on the process of internal change within Africa. How much the Soviet leadership in fact worries about new Western bases in Southern Africa or a new military alliance in the South Atlantic is beyond determination. But Soviet analysts mention the problems often enough, and presumably in this instance they recognize the link between their internal and external stakes in Africa.

Third, and I think only third, the Soviet Union has *offensive national concerns* in the area. It is in this category that our chief anxiety—the security of the Cape trade route—resides. To this one could add the Soviet interest in being able to menace *our* hydrographic, oceanographic, and satellite tracking activities, or perhaps someday our exploitation of marine resources. But the core concern remains the trade route. At one level, this concern makes considerable sense—not only because the great bulk of oil imported by Western Europe and the United States plies this route but also because Admiral Gorshkov regularly points this fact out when he writes about sea power. And, indeed, in the context of the Ogaden war, Soviet writers have commented on the license Western powers claim in the name of preserving their unhindered sway over the sea lanes. Rejecting their right to meddle in local instabilities in order to maintain command of the ocean ways is not, granted, equal to threatening their free use. Still, a question is being raised about positions the West regards with extreme jealousy.

At another level, however, the concern should be weighed against several offsetting factors. One, if the Soviet Union is determined to interrupt the flow of oil to the West, it would be far more effective to stop up the Straits of Hormuz. (True, the Soviet Union is always interested in redundant capabilities and, true, stopping up the Straits of Hormuz does not permit differentiating oil flows to Western Europe from those to Japan, should this be in the Soviet interest.) Two, interrupting the flow of oil is an act of war and not something the Soviet Union is likely to treat as just another way to apply diplomatic or political pressure. Three, the Soviet Union has the capability to interrupt the flow of oil but not the staying power to keep it interrupted over a period of more than a few months. Four, and most important, the Soviet Union's own large merchant marine and fishing fleet constitute counter-hostages.

Last, and least important, the Soviet Union has *offensive strategic concerns* in this area. Someday, for example, it may want to use the South Atlantic to hide its new generation of

[169]

submarines bearing long-range underwater-launched ballistic missiles; facilities on the west coast of Africa would then come in handy. Or, someday still farther into the future, were the Soviet Union to achieve effective ASW against the American strategic submarine force, including *Trident* (!), airfields on this side of Africa would become enormously important. Less in the realm of fantasy, the Soviet Union would doubtless like to see the Western powers deprived of all military infrastructure on either littoral.

What the implications of all this are can only be guessed—and then only in part. I would like to suggest three. First, if the hierarchy of Soviet concerns is roughly in this order, the threat to our fundamental interests is less immediate and profound than some people are quick to argue. Second, and on the other hand, no matter what the order or blend of these concerns, the Soviet Union now has an external stake in Africa that guarantees a competition between our two countries for the acquisition of facilities along both littorals. Should the occasion arise, it probably also guarantees that each will work to deprive the other side of facilities. The competition seems all the more certain given the Soviet determination to project military power before it has organic support (i.e., oilers, repair ships, and other auxiliaries); the lack of support ships increases its dependency on shore facilities, a dependency that is considerably greater than our own.

The third implication comes not so much from the catalogue of Soviet concerns in Africa as from its concerns elsewhere in the Indian Ocean. When considering the ways the two sides worry about military developments in the Indian Ocean nothing is so evident as the discrepancy in focus. Each is worrying on different planes. Thus, the United States tends to focus on those areas where the Soviet Union is most actively building its long-range military infrastructure, one of which appears to be Africa. The Soviet Union, on the other hand, tends to focus on the resurrection and extension of the American infrastructure in the Indian Ocean, which leads it to a preoccupation with the area's Pacific reaches (plus Diego Garcia). We fuss continually about Berbera (or did until the Ogaden War) Socotra, Port Louis, Conakry, and now Soviet naval activity in Angola. They worry about the revival of ANZUS, the welcome again extended to American missile-cruisers in Cockburn Sound, the modernization of Learmouth base, the provision for joint patrolling, and so on. We feature the threat to the Cape trade route; they the link Diego Garcia forms between CENTO (Chahbarhar and Bandar Abbas in Southern Iran) and North West Cape (in Australia). We see Soviet military power cropping up along the coast of Africa. They focus on the network of naval and air bases stretching from Oman, Bahrein, Mahé Island, and Réunion to the Ocean's other side. We think about Soviets and Arabs. They about Americans, French, British, South Africans, and Chinese. The list could be much longer but there is no purpose in drawing it out. The point is that we have quite different perceptions of what is happening in the Indian Ocean and, therefore, of the growth in the Soviet Union's East African military facilities.

By featuring the military dimension, I have inevitably had less to say about China's part in Soviet concerns. The inattention, however, is not meant to suggest that China matters less to the Soviet Union, only that the competition with the United States has its own specific and separate qualities. Indeed the Soviet Union's problem with the Chinese remains a major distraction with more than a faint echo in the military sphere. That is, a part of the Soviet strategic stake in the Indian Ocean, including the facilities that it wishes along the East African littoral, has to do with the military requirements of its own containment policy. Since clearly a primary objective of the Soviet Union's proposed Asian security system as well as of its diplomacy toward Japan is to ring China with a constellation of states keyed on the Chinese threat, the flow of Soviet naval power into these regions constitutes a logical military counterpart. Moreover, within Africa itself, the competition with China has always involved arms and the issue of armed violence, sometimes in the two sides' struggle for influence among the area's national liberation movements, at other times in their contributions to insurgencies within independent African states.

Until Angola, the discrepancy between these two concerns was great: Defending against China as such involved an entirely different magnitude of military power than the marginal (military) resources applied to the competition in Africa. But Angola represents a sharp escalation in the level of force the Soviet Union is prepared (and allowed) to commit in an area like this. As such, it marks an important transition in the competition with China, for now the Soviet Union emerges as the power better endowed to aid Africa in the next stage of its struggle against the white regimes of the south. Africa has reached the point where it needs patrons capable of supplying a major war effort against the regime in Salisbury and perhaps even naval protection against a major South African attack on exposed states like Mozambique. Since only the Soviet Union can perform at both levels, it has a growing advantage over the Chinese.

Even sooner, however, the competition itself had undergone a basic transformation. In the early 1960s when the conflict with China erupted, China stood as something of a revolutionary conscience, exposing Soviet concessions to imperialism, and threatening constantly to outflank the Soviet Union on the left. At the time the conflict was focused primarily on Africa's

[172]

revolutionary groups and "radical" regimes. Since the early 1970s, however, the Chinese have extended, indeed, converted their preoccupation from a concern with the Soviet betrayal of revolution to a conventional fear of the Soviet Union's broader ambitions. In the 1960s the Chinese appeared to make areas like Africa the arena both of its struggle against imperialism, still regarded as the primary foe, and of its campaign against Soviet heresies. By the 1970s Soviet heresies were no longer the only or even the central issue, nor was imperialism any longer the primary foe; the Soviet Union was. Apparently convinced that the Soviet leaders were not merely faint-hearted revolutionaries but an aggressive, ambitious group who threatened the security of China and many other countries, the Chinese set about to impede Soviet policy at every turn. If this meant collaborating with the most conservative elements, as China did in effect in Angola, then so be it. In the process, not merely were Third World regions like Africa turned into simply another site of a universal crusade against Soviet policy, no more or less significant than, say, Europe, but the Chinese strategy assumed an essentially expedient character.

For the Soviet Union, China now emerged less as a purer revolutionary competitor, threatening to siphon off the most restless parts of the national liberation movement, and more as one of the great conservative forces in international politics—an implacable opponent of détente and an arch foe of the Soviet Union's growing global role. While it is a mistake to make China the principal explanation for Soviet initiatives in Angola and southern Africa, as some have done, the strange mix that contemporary Chinese policy is between John Foster Dulles and Che Guevara clearly occupies a great deal of the Soviet Union's attention and it provides the Soviet leaders with an important additional reason for wanting to forestall Chinese influence wherever possible. In this respect, Angola, Rhodesia, and Namibia offer excellent opportunities.

II. The Soviet Union in Africa's Impending Crises

So much—in brief—for the broad basic Soviet-American military competition in Africa. The immediate question is how this may affect their roles in Africa's future (military) conflicts: how the competition may penetrate the crises, the crises accentuate the competition.

I think the place to start is with the Angolan War. It has a great deal to teach, both for the parallels with crises to come and even more for the parallels that almost certainly will never arise. These begin with the two most striking aspects of Soviet involvement: On the one hand, how decisive Soviet (and Cuban) intervention was—never had the Soviet Union or its allies decided with their military power the outcome of a third-party conflict, never in the Soviet Union's history. On the other hand, it is equally striking, if true, how awry the original premises of the Soviet Union's success were. There is not much need to elaborate the first point. The Soviet Union and Cuba (on its own initiative and not in response to Soviet dictate) came promptly and generously to the aid of their friends, the MPLA. They, or at least the Soviets, did so nine months before independence, and by August 1975 they had already begun the bold transfer of Cuban troops. Thus, from the very start they had moved swiftly and seemingly without hesitation to ensure a triumph that otherwise probably could not have been. That by itself would seem extremely portentous.

The second point, however, complicates the picture. It is important, I think, that the Soviet Union launched itself into the Angolan War probably never dreaming that its role would turn out to be either so decisive ór so obtrusive. Instead, in all probability, when the Soviet Union set its course in the spring and summer of 1975, it thought Angola's future had been predetermined in Lisbon by the progressive officers of the Armed Forces Movement. In all likelihood, the Soviet leaders viewed their own role as secondary—as providing aid to keep their friends in the running, a push on behalf of elements basically congenial to leading figures within the AFM. By the time they discovered this was not the case, they were already in up to their ears. Even then they might have backed off had they faced a determined and visible American opposition or, more to the point, had the OAU in January condemned all outside interference. But the bankruptcy of American opposition and the action of the South Africans saved them the choice.

Whether wittingly or not, however, the Soviet initiative was an audacious departure from past behavior, and it must be seen as a sign that, in the right circumstances, the Soviet Union is ready to play a major part in Africa's struggles. It becomes critical then to know in how many other instances the circumstances are likely to be right.

My own answer is: In not very many, but the few that are right count enormously. In Angola, several crucial considerations prevailed: (1) the Soviet Union was not intervening against a legitimate government; (2) it was not jeopardizing its relations with any African country whose goodwill it prized; (3) it was not risking a heavy direct involvement that could not be easily terminated were the war to drag on or turn out badly; (4) it was not risking a direct confrontation with the United States, not as matters unfolded; and, most important, (5) it was not acting against the will of most African states.

The obvious thing about these considerations is that they

apply equally to Rhodesia, but with a partial qualification: Should the transition to black rule erupt in civil war, again the Soviet Union will be on the right side, again its help will be valued, again it will not face any effective American opposition, and again it will be acting in basic concert with most of the OAU. Setting aside considerations beyond Africa, the Soviet Union has every incentive to bankroll and join a liberation war in Zimbabwe.

But, while most African states welcome the Soviet Union's military assistance, few of them appear as interested in having direct Soviet involvement. In fact, according to Colin Legum, the front-line presidents are agreed to keep the forces of external powers out of the conflict; and the Soviet Union is likely to observe this circumscription, at least as long as the front-line presidents have the sanction of the rest of Africa. This still leaves room for Soviet or Cuban troops to fill in the rear, to maintain Mozambique's defenses and free its forces for the war in Zimbabwe. And it still leaves room for the Soviet Union to supply the war effort, which, even if filtered through OAU auspices, will earn it considerable credit.

Thus, while in any future war in southern Africa the Soviet Union is likely to be the only outside power to whom the combatants can turn for critical military support, whether they do will depend on whether they have a choice, that is, on whether they have successfully fashioned their own Joint African Military Force (JAMF), clearly their preferred course. Again, all of the front-line presidents, including President Machel of Mozambique, would rather mobilize their defense from among African states than accept a direct and major Soviet role, and by all indications they will first try to do so. If they fail, however, or if the conflict escalates to open war between South Africa and base countries like Mozambique, then almost certainly the greater power of the Soviet Union

[176]

will be invited in. Machel, for one, apparently believes that in any large-scale conflict with South Africa—whether in the course of the struggle over Zimbabwe or in the next stage in the assault on South Africa itself—his country will have to secure the alliance of a major power. But, for the moment, his colleagues have persuaded him to proceed without it.

For the Soviet Union, another constraint probably also operates, and this is the damaging effect that crude and large-scale meddling in the Rhodesian conflict may have on East-West relations. The other surprise in Angola, from the Soviet perspective, was the backlash that the intervention stirred in the United States. Perhaps partially because they did not expect to be so much out front, the Soviet leaders almost certainly did not expect their actions in Angola to prejudice détente so. Until the very end they appeared puzzled by the storm generated in the United States. While tending to attribute this in large part to artificial stimulation, blaming Kissinger in particular, they nevertheless were keen to limit the damage done. Something of the same concern is likely to exist in the Rhodesia case. By itself this will scarcely dissuade the Soviet Union from intervening, but it may influence the nature of Soviet intervention; it may reinforce the effect of other constraints produced within Africa.

In the meantime, while the Soviet Union resents and opposes the diplomatic pre-eminence that the honest broker's role gives the United States in the Rhodesian negotiations, it would be too simple to say that the Soviet Union opposes any negotiated settlement. It is equally dubious to argue that the Soviet Union wants a prolonged guerrilla struggle, seeing this as the surest way to the victory of a radicalized pro-Soviet guerrilla movement. Certainly the Soviet Union would like to see its own influence in the area increased and the United States' diminished; indeed, given the history of American

[177]

policy in southern Africa, it probably regards this as its right. But the Soviet Union sees more to be gained from almost every perspective if a negotiated settlement can be achieved, *provided* it is on the terms of the Patriotic Front. Unlike Angola, the Soviet Union does not have a history of involvement with the Zimbabwe guerrilla movement. Unlike Angola, none of the principal groups has a clear ideological orientation on which the Soviet Union can count. And unlike Angola, it has more to lose if the opposition is divided and left to wage separate wars. The important consideration, however, is that the settlement be on the Patriotic Front's terms, the more radical the better. It is for this reason that the Soviet Union consistently rejects the American appeal for an "African solution."

Having noted the constraints on the Soviet role in Rhodesia, we should not underestimate the room this still leaves for Soviet involvement nor the readiness of the Soviet Union to become involved. Soviet commentary has been from the beginning that the path of peaceful settlement is "discredited" and that only the "armed struggle" remains. Alone in the Rhodesian case have they taken this line. Elsewhere, whether in Angola before the civil war, in the Horn, within Ethiopia, or in Spanish Sahara, the line has always been "mediation" and avoiding the "internationalization" of conflict. Soviet diplomats will on occasion explain away the stronger language as a concession granted Joshua Nkomo, but we have every right to assume that the Soviet leaders are prepared to stand behind it. Thus, if the negotiations for an alternative to the "internal settlement" disintegrate into war, the Soviet Union is likely to lend far-reaching support. Whether they or the Cubans would actually fight the war is another matter, but not to be ruled out, not, in particular, if it is at African urging. In any case, Soviet behavior cannot be predicted in advance, since it will

[178]

depend not only on the role the Africans will want the Soviet Union to play and the role the Americans will allow them to play but also on the status of the Soviet Union's other African entanglements. It will also depend on the prospect of an early and relatively easy success. Almost certainly the Soviet leaders themselves do not yet know how they will act in the event.

Again, however, Angola and Rhodesia should not mislead us. Africa's crises do not inevitably open the way to Soviet influence, nor do they always enable the Soviet Union to bring its growing military might to bear. In Shaba province, for example, where virtually none of the circumstances of Angola prevailed, the Soviets remained carefully aloof from events. Whatever contribution the Soviet Union and Cuba may have made to the pre-battle training or servicing of the Shaba rebels, once they crossed the border (1) to wage war against a legitimate black African government (2) without the sympathy of the remainder of black Africa, and (3) with limited prospects of success (4) in part because a series of outside powers were prepared to come to Kinshasa's aid, the Soviet Union did everything it could to convince the West (and Africa) that its hands were clean. Had the rebels succeeded, the Soviet Union would doubtless have embraced them—but not before.

The Horn of Africa is still another instance, a special case whose implications are lodged somewhere between those of Angola and those of the Shaba incursion. It has been a curious mixture of success and failure for the Soviet Union, of realpolitik and naiveté, of caution and assertiveness. The Soviet Union started by supporting two promising revolutions, that is, the Ethiopian revolution added to the Somalian revolution, trusting in the force of their common socialist aspirations to control historic antagonisms and ambitions, and struggling to perform the role of mediator. It ended by losing

[179]

its position in one and vastly enlarging its place in the other, largely by making a wholesale military commitment to Ethiopia's victory in a war the Soviet Union tried and failed to prevent.

What is to be said about the experience? First, on our own ability to draw the implications: For most of the recent period the focus of our concerns has not turned out to be well-chosen, and we should be duly modest in predicting those of the future. At a minimum, simple projections and simple apprehensions based on simple notions of a strategic competition between the United States and the Soviet Union in this region, it seems to me, grow less and less appropriate.

We ought not to forget that scarcely a year before the recent war our chief worry centered on a Somali-Ethiopian conflict that might produce a Soviet-American confrontation, as we rallied to the Ethiopian side and they to the other. Moreover, to the extent that we thought we knew what drove Soviet policy in the area, we assumed that it was a narrowly conceived quest for facilities to service a burgeoning military presence abroad. The Soviet Union's primary interest, many argued, was in Berbera and, with half a chance, in similar facilities in Djibouti.

Once the Soviet Union was cast out of Somalia, a variety of commentators concluded that this represented on the Soviet part a carefully calculated reversal of alliances. Ethiopia being the more attractive prize, the Soviet leaders accordingly had sacrificed their position in Somalia to seize it. Or, in the minds of some prepared to follow this line of analysis still further, the alliance with Ethiopia and the ensuing war represented a plan by which the Soviet Union would come to command all of the strategic stakes in the region. Simply stated, the road to Berbera and beyond passed by way of Addis.

The flaws in our earlier formulations stemmed from the

tendency to reduce the considerations behind Soviet policy to the strategic. In truth, Soviet policy has responded neither first nor only to strategic considerations. Rather, the impulse propelling policy seems to be a complicated combination of concerns and calculations. This is the second point to be made. No doubt the Soviet leadership gave and continues to give great weight to the acquisition of military facilities. But the urge to acquire facilities does not alone explain Soviet choices. Part of the explanation also belongs to the forces of change in which it believes and which it supports. The Soviet Union has been deeply attracted to the Ethiopian revolution. From every indication, Soviet observers consider it a profounder, purer, and more durable transformation of a society than almost any other in Africa.

The argument is not that the Soviet Union chose the Ethiopian revolution over the Somalian revolution because it believed more in the first. On the contrary, it chose both and fervently hoped that it would not be forced against its will to elect one over the other. (The point is, however, that, when forced to choose, it did not, as the simple strategic analysis would logically imply, rally to the Somalis.) In choosing both, the Soviet Union was also responding to its faith in the transcendent strength of revolutionary (socialist) aspirations. Evidently the Soviet leaders genuinely believed that the commitment of these two regimes to socialism had created, or should have created, a fraternity more powerful than the historic and cultural forces setting them against one another and, thanks to it, that they had reason to think they could succeed in mediating the conflict.

It was, as things turned out, a misplaced faith, based on a misjudgment of the situation, which leads to my third point. By and large, Soviet policy in Africa is as much subject to and victim of preconceptions, shallow analysis, and decisions made

[181]

at the top by people unpersuaded by, even indifferent to, their own experts as that of any other country. Over the years the Soviet Union's appreciation of the complexity and uncertainty in the process of change *within* African societies has matured considerably. The same cannot yet be said of its appreciation of the subtler and more intricate aspects of relations between these societies. So, when Soviet Africanists, Third World specialists, and diplomats with experience in the area warned of the deeper flowing forces in Somali-Ethiopian relations, as some apparently did, the cautioning made too little of an impression.

Thus, Soviet involvement stemmed not from a careful and accurate assessment of the situation in the Horn and the systematic implementation of a policy dictated by this original assessment. More than anything, the Soviet Union was drawn by events from one step to the next and, ultimately, found itself facing a set of policy choices distant from those anticipated at the outset. Not only has Soviet action in the Horn been far from a component in some larger African design, it has never had its own design even in the specific instance. The experience there reinforces the impression that Soviet involvement in Africa's instabilities is part of an inchoate rather than conscious pattern—an important distinction because it says something about the single-mindedness with which the Soviet Union will approach future conflicts in the area.

The fourth and fifth points relate to the character of Soviet involvement. Nothing in the sequence of Soviet initiatives contradicts the general cautiousness of earlier Soviet policy. Neither in relation to the preferences of the vast majority of African states nor in relation to the risks inherent in military interference did the Soviet Union behave recklessly. On the contrary, again, the Soviet sensitivity to the stand of OAU members was evident throughout. Similarly, the decision to mount massive assistance to the Ethiopian cause was apparently taken only after it became clear that the Somali offensive had been stopped and that a properly organized and equipped counteroffensive could drive the Somalis from their positions without enormous difficulty. Even so, throughout the escalation of Soviet aid, Soviet commentary betrayed a good deal of nervousness over the degree to which others on the outside would go in propping up the Somali effort.

The fifth point is somewhat different but not inconsistent with the last. Twice now the Soviet Union has successfully employed military force in Africa. It may not have intended to play this role when the story began in either the Angolan or the Ethiopian instance and it may not automatically prefer this role in advance the next time around, but there is no gainsaying the success that it has had nor the likelihood that the success has left its mark on Soviet calculations. The open question is whether the Soviet Union has learned lessons from these two episodes that it never intended to learn, dangerously inappropriate lessons about how easily and decisively force can be applied to African conflicts or how tolerant or hindered the American response will be. Or, on the other hand, whether the Soviet leadership attributes its success to the measured application of force and wisely selected opportunities, without underestimating the limits and risks inherent in military intervention.

Thus, however, crucial, southern Africa is not the only measure of our competition with the Soviet Union. Other situations, including other instabilities, have a different character and require that policy makers develop a highly refined notion of what our competition with the Soviet Union in Africa is all about. First, policy makers need to avoid oversimplifying Soviet objectives in this area and, therefore, miscasting our own. At one level, the Soviet Union indisputably is motivated by the desire to accumulate military facilities and prejudice our own. But, as the course of Soviet policy in the Horn demonstrates, that is not always the first or the primary objective of policy. (Had it been, the Soviet Union would have willingly sponsored war in the Horn and the Somali side in it. Instead, the Soviet Union obviously regrets the outbreak of war and the destruction of its position in Somalia.) The Soviet Union is also moved by the prospect of social and political transformations in this area that require longer-term and more subtle political investments than the crude manipulations of military force.

Second, policy makers need to be sensitive to the constraints imposed on the Soviet role in Africa, even in its crises, and, therefore, avoid assuming the burden of countering it at every turn. Too often, only the African area specialist makes this his or her premise and the rest of us work with stereotypes or simple models dominated by worst-case analysis. The course of African events, however, has not been easily manipulated from the outside, not even Africa's instabilities, and there is no reason to assume they will be in the future. Equally important, the Soviet leadership appears to recognize the complexity of African politics and is not likely to oversimplify its own opportunities in the area.

Third, policy makers need to calculate accurately the essential African dimension to the evolution of events and, therefore, resist viewing matters always or too soon from an East-West perspective. Africa has always had a way of defying our natural inclination to fit its crises into our global concerns. We get ourselves into the most trouble—as in the Congo in the early 1960s and in Angola more recently—by repressing this fact and mistranslating the clash of African interests into a contest between the Soviet Union and ourselves. When the rest of the world does not see it as such and, particularly, when Africa does not, we end by isolating ourselves from the Africans we most need to influence.

And, fourth, policy makers need to distinguish between our basic strategic competition with the Soviet Union and the problem we have with the Soviet Union in specific instances. Given the evolution of Soviet military power in general, it is inevitable that the United States will seek to maintain its own global military infrastructure. It is inevitable that wherever and whenever the Soviet Union gains new facilities or engages its military resources in some fashion we are going to be concerned and tempted, in the first instance, to devise some direct counter. But in Africa, particularly in southern Africa, rather than escalate matters to a direct issue between the two powers, we would be far wiser to make the solution a function of our own African policy—that is, to reduce the disabilities of our policy in this region. Since the Soviet role (and rewards) in this area clearly depend on the choices that the African nations feel they have or not, we would do best to protect their choices. This can only be done by facing squarely the imperative of black majority rule in all these countries, not in order to vie with the Soviet Union in applying our military power, but in order to return the competition to those frameworks in which we are better placed to carry on.

In sum, our strategic competition in Africa is broader, less immediate, and more involved than we often assume and essentially a function of our general strategic competition. Its mitigation will come only in revising or adjusting the overall relationship. But the challenge of dealing with the Soviet Union in Africa's crises is or can be a function of Africa's own peculiar complexities. It is very much in our interest to keep them as much separated as possible.

NOTES

1. By Soviet tally, ten African countries have now "proclaimed socialism as their goal and have started reshaping their social and economic relations along non-capitalist lines."

SIX

U.S. Options vis-à-vis South Africa

Andrew Nagorski

In southern Africa, the line between perceptions of political realities and the realities themselves is a hazy one at best; more often than not, the perceptions become a major component of the situation, influencing events in a very direct fashion. This has been particularly true for the region's ruling white minorities. Although Portugal's colonial wars were obviously unwinnable in the long run, it was not until the Portuguese military recognized that fact that the war effort finally collapsed. And in Rhodesia and South Africa, white perceptions of the degree of support or opposition for their cause in the West has been a crucial variable in the overall political equation.

After the victory of the Soviet-backed liberation group in Angola in early 1976, white Rhodesians began to acknowledge that the Western world's relationship with southern Africa had undergone a fundamental transformation; far fewer

[187]

illusions remained that the West would rush to their aid. The beginning of a similar process was soon evident in South Africa. Foreign Minister Pik Botha first sounded the theme in October 1976 when he was still his country's ambassador to Washington: South Africa, he told his countrymen, could not count on the West to come to its aid. In his 1977 New Year's address, Prime Minister John Vorster echoed Botha's words. "If . . . a Communist onslaught should be made against South Africa directly or under camouflage, then South Africa will have to face it alone and certain countries who profess to be anti-Communist will even refuse to sell arms to South Africa to beat off the attack."

But most South Africans did not—and still do not—believe either warning. The descendants of Dutch and British immigrants who arrived in South Africa from the seventeenth century onward, South Africa's ruling classes saw themselves, and were largely seen by others until the 1950s, as a snug Western enclave at the tip of Africa. Faithfully Christian, they staunchly opposed communism and governed themselves according to a Westminster model of parliamentary democracy. All this made it extremely difficult for them to understand that their exclusion of their country's black majority from political participation effectively placed them outside the post-World War II Western alliance systems.

It is doubtful that they still entirely accept this political fact of life. Although Vice President Walter Mondale spelled out the Carter administration's general views on southern Africa in strong terms during his Vienna meeting with Vorster in May 1977, there is still considerable question whether Vorster, Botha, and other South African officials really believe their own warnings about their country's isolation—or whether they simply feel it necessary gradually to wean South Africans away from the belief that the West will come down on their side in international forums. White South Africans freely acknowledge that Western support for their cause has seriously eroded since the first Soweto riots in June 1976; and they have reacted with defiance, largely supporting the government's sweeping crackdown on all opponents of apartheid in October 1977, shrugging off the death of Steve Biko, and awarding Vorster an overwhelming victory at the polls in November. But when the crunch comes, most of them continue to expect the Western powers—and the United States, in particular—to help defend them against what they see as the Communist-inspired black menace.

South African perceptions of the West are crucial to any discussion of U.S. options vis-à-vis southern Africa. The perceptions I am talking about are not only those of hardcore Afrikaners, although that element of the population expresses itself most openly on the subject. Many liberals, when questioned carefully beyond the point where they express their pessimism about the future, admit to the belief that they cannot imagine a day when the West would simply stand by impassively while the whites make their last stand. The rationale behind that reasoning is that South Africa is too valuable, both economically and strategically, for the West to abandon it to a Soviet-backed black regime. "Our mineral wealth is so vast that the Russians would cut their bloody right hands off to have this lot," says retired Rear Admiral Stefanus Biermann. "And if South Africa should fall into the hands of the Communists, they would control the whole Cape sea route."

Just as South African perceptions of the West are crucial to any discussion of U.S. options vis-à-vis South Africa, they are also crucial to any broader deliberations that include such relatively short-range issues as Rhodesia and Namibia, for the key to peace in the entire southern African region is South

Africa itself. In the case of Rhodesia, the country could not have so long survived the combination of external and internal pressures brought to bear upon it—U.N. economic sanctions that were imposed in 1966 and guerrilla attacks launched from Tanzania, Zambia, and later Mozambique—without a steady flow of military and civilian supplies across the South African-Rhodesian border. And the future of Namibia is totally dependent on South Africa's willingness to comply with U.N. demands that it relinquish its control of the territory. Known since the nineteenth century as South West Africa, the former German colony was designated a U.N. trust territory under South African administration. With the advent of independence in much of black Africa, however, pressures on South Africa mounted steadily. In a series of resolutions from 1968 onward, the United Nations demanded that South Africa grant independence to the territory and permit elections in which SWAPO, the militant black nationalist group that has been waging a guerrilla war against South African troops in Namibia, would be allowed to freely participate.

The goal of U.S. policy in both cases is an internationally sanctioned transition to majority rule. But no matter how difficult the transitions prove to be, the United States must not lose sight of the fact that the central problem of the region is the future of South Africa itself. The Kissingerian concept of "linkage"—the belief that the problem of South Africa should be largely ignored until the Rhodesian and Namibian issues are resolved—contains a fatal flaw: the assumption that events will stand still in South Africa while the other short-range regional issues are dealt with. Everything that has happened since the first Soweto riots in June 1976 proves that the exact opposite is happening. The resolution of South Africa's dilemma will certainly be long in coming, but the battle is already well underway and no other struggle is as important for Africa's future and its entire relationship with the United States and the rest of the Western world.

The United States, therefore, must seriously examine its options vis-à-vis South Africa. To do so, it must first analyze the rationale presented by Admiral Biermann and other white South Africans about the strategic and economic stakes involved. Is South Africa as important to the West as South Africans maintain; and, if so, have the South Africans correctly analyzed why it is important? This study will make the case that South Africa is important to the West, but for different reasons than those presented by the South Africans themselves. With that as a starting point, four main U.S. options will be discussed: (1) maintaining a hands-off policy toward the South African situation; (2) attempting to reform South African society by encouraging U.S. business interests in South Africa to exert pressures for change; (3) applying direct measures on South Africa in the form of political and economic sanctions against it; (4) providing financial and military assistance to the black liberation movements seeking the overthrow of the present regime.

U.S. INTERESTS IN SOUTH AFRICA

How important is South Africa to the West in economic terms? U.S. investments in South Africa amount to $1.67 billion or 1.18 percent of its total foreign investments, while U.S. annual trade with South Africa amounts to $2.27 billion or 1.05 percent of its total world trade (1976 figures). Britain is South Africa's major trading partner: Its investments in South Africa equal about $6 billion or 10 percent of its total foreign investment, while its annual trade with South Africa is also about $2.3 billion which accounts for about 2 percent of

[191]

its world trade. West Germany has usually been listed as South Africa's second largest trading partner, but recent import-export figures reveal that the United States has edged into second place, dropping Germany to third place. Its trade with South Africa is about $1.7 billion or 0.9 percent of its total world trade. Japan, France and Italy, the next highest trading partners of South Africa, have even smaller stakes on both a quantitative and a proportional basis. Therefore, only Britain can be described as a nation heavily dependent on South Africa in terms of trade and investment. That fact has been brought home by the failure of the Labour government to change Britain's economic relationship with South Africa after three years in office. Whatever discomfort such ties may cause, it appears that no British government can afford to pay the political price of taking action to drastically curtail British business interests in South Africa, thereby adding to Britain's unemployment problems and its general economic troubles. The conventional wisdom is that any government that did so would almost certainly be voted out of office.

The United States—and, theoretically at least, France and West Germany—are not operating under such constraints. South Africa's economic importance must be put into perspective: it makes up a relatively small part of their overall trade and investment picture. A more serious consideration is the importance of its natural resources. At the moment, South Africa and Rhodesia provide the West with 50 percent of its chrome and 75 percent of its platinum. South Africa alone provides the West with 60 percent of its vanadium and 30 percent of its manganese, and it supplies the world with a major portion of its gold, diamonds and uranium. As high as those percentages are, many industrialists concede that in most cases alternate sources of the raw materials South Africa provides to the West could be found. This would involve considerable planning, new investment and, above all, a conscious decision to do so. But it could be done.

This does not mean that South Africa is not an important economic power; it is. And in purely economic terms it is perfectly natural that Western nations should seek to tap its formidable resources. But to say, as many South Africans do, that its minerals are absolutely critical to the West is an overstatement.

The South African argument about its strategic role is similarly overstated. There is no denying that the expanded Soviet naval presence in the Indian Ocean has raised serious questions about its ultimate intentions—questions that no one has adequately answered. But the argument put forth by Admiral Biermann and others that South Africa is a vital link in the Western defense system is highly debatable. A case in point: the South Africans maintain that the West needs to have access to port facilities on the South African coast. But since 1967 U.S. Navy ships have observed a voluntary boycott of South African ports, despite an open invitation to use their facilities.

More significantly, the entire "defense of the Cape sea route" argument is based on a faulty assumption—namely, that the Russians would have to control the Cape itself to cut off the West's supply lines. The Cape route is an extremely long one and, as one top former Pentagon official concedes, the Russians could attempt to cut that supply line in any number of places. However, the most crucial consideration that the South African propagandists conveniently overlook is that an attempt by the Soviet Union to interdict traffic anywhere along that route could only be taken as an act of war. Thus, even a scenario which envisions the takeover of South Africa by a pro-Soviet black government does not automatically lead to the conclusion that Western Europe's vital trade route would be suddenly severed. That is not a decision which could be taken lightly by the leadership in the Kremlin.

Once again, as in the case of South Africa's economy, none of this is meant to dismiss South Africa's strategic role; it simply must be subjected to a critical analysis. Although the United States quite visibly does not feel the need to use South African port facilities, a sudden shift in South Africa that would be followed by the opening of port facilities to the Soviet Navy would be a matter of serious concern. Its impact on the global balance of power would have to be carefully weighed. But there is no convincing evidence that even such worst-case scenarios would lead to the results predicted by the South Africans themselves.

South Africa's real importance to the United States may be much less strategic and economic than political. For much of the Third World—and black Africa, in particular—South Africa is seen as the acid test of the new administration. A continuation of old policies—that is, mildly reprimanding South Africa about apartheid in international forums while opposing almost all concrete actions against it—would be seen as an indication that the Carter administration's pledge to chart new directions in foreign policy amounts to nothing but rhetoric. Its stance on human rights would be dismissed as mere propaganda, and any claim that the administration would make about being guided by moral principles in its conduct of foreign policy would be the object of derision.

That would seriously undermine the administration's plans to forge new ties with the Third World. It would almost certainly insure that the Third World would continue to ally itself on many major issues with the Communist nations in showdowns at the United Nations. It would seriously decrease the chances of making substantial progress in the North-South talks. And in the long run, it could also reverse or at least slow down the trend towards the expansion of trade between the United States and black Africa—a trend that has already made black Africa far more important to this country in terms of trade than South Africa.

But even if the South African analysis is correct that economic and strategic stakes in South Africa outweigh those political stakes for the United States, the final conclusion of that argument does not necessarily follow. The South Africans maintain that once they have proved the importance of their country to the West in those terms, the Western powers will see they have no choice but to back the present government. According to this reasoning, only white rule can insure a pro-Western government.

There are plenty of reasons to question that simplistic conclusion. Totally disregarding moral considerations for the moment, a much more convincing case can be made for the argument that the way to avoid having South Africa ultimately taken over by a pro-Soviet black government is for the United States to ally itself firmly with those forces seeking the overthrow of the present system. In terms of realpolitik, a de facto alliance with South Africa simply does not make sense any more. A brief examination of the events of the last few years reveals the dangers of accepting the narrow thesis that is being put forward by the South Africans today.

Until recently, U.S. administrations did in essence buy the South African line of reasoning. Economic and strategic considerations far outweighed political considerations, and the assumption, as spelled out in NSSM 39, was that the best way to protect those interests was to maintain ties with the white-controlled states of southern Africa. That thinking did not change drastically even after the 1974 Lisbon coup and the subsequent rapid Portuguese withdrawal from Mozambique and Angola, which caught American policy makers completely by surprise. It was not until the Cubans intervened in Angola that Kissinger began seriously to question any of the assumptions about U.S. policy in the region. The ill-fated Angolan rescue operation was the immediate reaction, and the Kissinger speech in Lusaka in April 1976, outlining a new U.S. commitment to majority rule in Rhodesia, was the first serious step toward redefining the American role in southern Africa.

In examining the chain of events that have followed the Lisbon coup—the Frelimo takeover in Mozambique, the MPLA victory in Angola, the growing militancy of the Nkomo-Mugabe faction in Rhodesia, and the Soweto riots within South Africa itself—the South Africans and many Westerners see an alarming trend: the spread of black rule, they assert, is leading to a corresponding growth in Soviet influence in Africa. An area of the world that was once solidly pro-Western now looks as though it all may eventually be dominated by governments indebted to Moscow. Even many Westerners who have opposed the white regimes in principle in the past are beginning to have their doubts about whether they are not in fact playing into Soviet hands.

That is precisely the kind of thinking that the South Africans—most notably such propaganda fronts as the "Club of Ten"—are feverishly trying to encourage. But even in looking at the conflict purely in East-West terms, a totally different conclusion can be reached about the lessons the West should learn from Mozambique and Angola as it tries to formulate a policy toward South Africa. By considering narrow strategic and economic interests to be of primary importance, the United States lost any chance of playing a constructive and effective role in a post-independence Mozambique and Angola and insured that the new governments would at the very least be extremely distrustful of its motives. Without much real effort, the Soviet Union could easily portray itself as the benefactor of liberation movements and a dedicated opponent of white racist regimes. Our history of maintaining an ambiguous stance on Rhodesia has also hurt our chances of bringing about a peaceful settlement there this late in the game—and a failure to achieve a peaceful settlement can only lead to the installation of a more militant black government once the Smith regime falls.

The danger of narrowly defining American self-interest is even greater when it comes to South Africa. Acceptance of the South African argument means that one accepts the assumption that white minority rule can continue indefinitely there—that, whatever the political costs, the United States will protect its strategic and economic interests by maintaining the old de facto alliance with South Africa. But fully recognizing the vast differences between South Africa and the rest of the region, I would suggest that the lesson of Angola, Mozambique, and Rhodesia is that white minority rule cannot survive indefinitely anywhere in Africa. Therefore, anything that appears to smack of an alliance between the United States and even the strongest of the white states is not only morally wrong but a grievous political miscalculation. It multiplies the chances of losing the very strategic and economic interests the United States is seeking to defend by lining up on the side of the losers; the ultimate winners will once again have nowhere to turn for support but to the Soviet Union. And whether that support is significant or not, by the time they do get into power they will feel indebted to just one side. We must not let the specter of a Soviet threat stampede us into repeating the mistakes of the past.

[197]

U.S. Options

Now, a look at the specific options.

Option 1—that is, maintaining a hands-off policy toward the South African situation—was spelled out in a *Washington Post* column (March 1, 1977) by Joseph Kraft. "Except for the good-guy impulse so brilliantly articulated by UN ambassador Andrew Young, it is hard to see why Washington should thrust itself more deeply into that mess," he writes. "Reason, on the contrary, suggests staying on the sidelines now the better to help later." Kraft does go on to say that "the chief American need in Africa is to avoid a tie with the losing cause of the white regimes." But he then concludes: "Lending further support to the black cause builds up expectations this country will not fulfill when it comes to the crunch in the Republic of South Africa. . . . This country cannot satisfy black aspirations in Africa soon. . . . As to showing American idealism, the best way to do that in Africa is to hold aloof for the time being so that when the smash-up comes this country can use its good offices to soften the impact."

Kraft's argument reflects a deep-seated impulse in American thinking—a fear of foreign entanglements. That impulse has frequently done battle with the other strain in American foreign policy—the desire to impose American values and American solutions on foreign countries. Paradoxically, those two seemingly contradictory impulses have co-existed throughout American history, with one occasionally gaining the ascendancy over the other but never quite eliminating it. The immediate post-Vietnam era gave a strong boost to those advocating disengagement from foreign trouble spots. However, the present administration's advocacy of morality in foreign policy, while apparently attempting to avoid any rash

[198]

new military ventures, suggests that neither impulse has been allowed to overly dominate the other. And, I would argue that in regard to South Africa this is a sensible approach. Contrary to the Kraft argument, I maintain that a hands-off policy is neither plausible nor desirable in political or moral terms.

First of all, neutrality is not a viable option given the U.S. involvement in South Africa to date. The Carter administration is currently faced with several major decisions: what attitude to take toward U.S. investments in South Africa and U.S. banks loans to South Africa, and what its position should be in the United Nations and other international forums now that it has gone along with the imposition of an arms embargo. Should it support the next step that many Third World nations are already pushing for: the imposition of economic sanctions? Those decisions cannot be avoided, and whatever is decided will be seen as a direct indication of American intentions. A refusal to take any position on the subject of U.S. investments in itself would be widely interpreted as a continuation of past policies. And "staying on the sidelines" is out of the question when it comes to votes on the South African issue in the United Nations; even abstaining on key votes where we might have cast vetoes in the past would be interpreted as a declaration of policy.

Most importantly, the Kraft argument breaks down by attempting "to avoid a tie with the losing cause of the white regimes" while maintaining a hands-off policy. That tie already exists: U.S. investments and trade with South Africa may be a small part of the overall American picture, but it is very important to the South Africans themselves. And the U.S. refusal to go along with U.N. resolutions seeking to isolate South Africa politically and economically has played a major role in keeping up South African morale and its determination not to be pressured into making major changes

[199]

in its apartheid policies. Given that past political history and present economic involvement, a hands-off policy would inevitably greatly encourage the South Africans and tremendously disappoint the Third World nations which have been eagerly awaiting a new U.S. position. Under those circumstances, it would hardly be surprising if the United States were seen as once again espousing the NSSM 39 philosophy with all its faulty assumptions. Just as the growing polarization within South Africa itself makes it increasingly difficult for either blacks or whites to "stay on the sidelines" there, the pressures building up in the international arena make it difficult for any nation—and impossible for a superpower like the United States—to feign noninvolvement. As a nation, the United States must face up to that fact.

But even if one accepts the Kraft premise that somehow it would be possible to maintain a hands-off policy without appearing to back the South Africans, is such a position defensible in moral terms? Up to this point, I have largely avoided any discussion of the moral issues involved in the South African situation, partly because they are readily apparent to most observers and partly because it puts the discussion on an emotional plane. But without indulging in shrill rhetoric, I think it is both possible and necessary to mention at least briefly the morality question. Starting from the assumption that there are certain extraordinary cases in history where a neutral stance is unacceptable in moral terms— Nazi Germany is the most obvious example—I maintain that South Africa qualifies as one of those cases. Why South Africa and not any number of other nations which also routinely violate human rights? The answer is that there is one fundamental difference that sets South Africa apart: Since the days of the Third Reich, no other modern society—however reprehensible, brutal or racist in practice—has deliberately constructed an elaborate system based purely on the tenets of racism. South Africa has. And if the United States wishes to claim any commitment to moral principle, a hands-off policy is no more a viable moral option than it is a viable political option.

One final point: Kraft does not consider the possibility that the United States might at least attempt to prevent "the smash-up" he predicts in South Africa, i.e., an all-out race war. There is no way of knowing at this point whether any U.S. policy can realistically be expected to avert a massive racial confrontation. But it would be both politically and morally irresponsible not to use whatever means there are at our disposal to attempt to bring about a peaceful solution. Not only would an all-out race war be catastrophic for South Africa itself, it would inevitably exacerbate American racial tensions. Both whites and blacks in the United States would demand to know why the government had done nothing to prevent the South African violence, and in such an atmosphere of distrust and bitterness the administration would find it extremely difficult to offer its "good offices," as Kraft suggests.

Just as accepting the first option would allow the impulse to avoid foreign entanglements to overly dominate the moralistic impulse in U.S. foreign policy, acceptance of the fourth option—providing financial and military assistance to black liberation movements—would do the exact opposite. The reasoning behind such a move would be that the United States not only must avoid backing the wrong or losing side, but must directly support those who will ultimately emerge as the winners. When posed in such simple terms, the logic appears to have a certain plausibility. Under closer scrutiny, however, the dangers of such a policy become obvious.

By choosing to provide black liberation groups with funds and arms, the United States would be placing itself in the position of attempting to impose a specific solution on South Africa. Aside from the important fact that this would in all likelihood be a violent solution, this is something that very few South African whites or blacks would find acceptable. Even the most militant blacks declare that the exact nature of the solutions to South Africa's problems must be worked out by the South Africans themselves. They are seeking U.S. support for the concept of a multiracial system based on participation by all groups in the political process, but they are not asking the United States to draw up a blueprint for that society. That is their own job.

But the most compelling reason to reject option 4 is that it would force the United States into the position of choosing between the various black South African groups and movements. U.S. policy makers would be faced with the task of deciding whether to support Gatsha Buthelezi and his tribal-based leadership, the exiles of the African National Congress (ANC) and of the Pan-Africanist Congress (PAC), or any combination of new organizations led by young militants from Soweto and other black townships. "That would get us back into an Angola or Vietnam situation," warns one top U.S. official. "Our job is not to choose between groups but to try to get all the groups involved in the political process." That definition of U.S. objectives seems eminently reasonable.

Given such a definition, the debate about U.S. policy vis-à-vis South Africa narrows down to an examination of options 2 and 3 or some variation of them.

During the last presidential campaign, Jimmy Carter appeared to favor option 2—attempting to reform South African society by encouraging U.S. business interests in South Africa to exert pressures for change. He declared in an interview with Johannesburg's *Financial Mail:* "American businessmen can be a constructive force, achieving racial justice within South Africa. Economic development, investment commitment, and the use of economic leverage against what is, after all, a government system of repression within South Africa seems to me the only way to achieve racial justice there."

That kind of statement reflects the belief that, with proper guidance, Western investment in South Africa can help raise living standards of blacks and gradually force the political system to begin responding to black aspirations. Any pull-out of Western capital is rejected on the grounds that the people who will be hurt most by such a move would be the very people the West is supposedly concerned about helping— South Africa's black laborers. Without Western investment, the present economic slowdown would be transformed into a major depression, leading to massive lay-offs of black unskilled and semi-skilled workers.

Examining the question of British involvement in South Africa,[1] Professor Merle Lipton of Sussex University has cogently argued that point of view. "Blacks have been and are gaining from growth," she writes, "and . . . growth is in some, though not all, ways undermining apartheid." While admitting that the ratio of black to white wages actually widened during the period from 1948 to 1970 when the South African economy was steadily expanding, she asserts that roughly from 1970 onwards economic growth and the rapid pace of industrialization began to work in favor of the black population, leading to a significant narrowing of the gap between white and black wages.

"In gold-mining—which has the most scandalous gap—the ratio of white to black wages narrowed from 20 to 1 in 1969 to 11.9 to 1 in 1974," she writes. "Between 1971 and 1975, the ratio narrowed from 6 to 1 to 4.7 to 1 in manufacturing; from

6.9 to 1 to 4.9 to 1 in construction; from 4.2 to 1 to 3.8 to 1 in commerce; and from 6.2 to 1 to 4.6 to 1 in government service."

Lipton argues that this trend will continue for several reasons. The result of economic expansion is that more blacks are moving into semi-skilled and skilled jobs, thereby changing occupational patterns. The government is shifting its wage policy, urging businessmen to raise black wages faster than white wages. And black trade unions have been revived, leading to increased black bargaining power. Lipton claims that the final point may be most significant, and the experience blacks gain in bargaining for economic rights will be of immense help as they seek to win political rights as well.

The underlying assumption behind all such arguments put forth by advocates of option 2 is that there is still plenty of time for evolutionary change in South Africa. They simply refuse to believe that the Soweto violence and its aftermath signify a major turning point in South African history. "Most predictions about the course of events in South Africa have proved wrong," Lipton writes. "There were endless false predictions of revolution in the 1960s."

But the Soweto riots were a watershed; they revolutionized black political thinking. Over and over again, even the most moderate blacks in South Africa now insist that minor modifications of the present system and slow evolutionary change will no longer be accepted by the black population. Putting faith in such developments, they assert, will insure that any hope of peaceful change will disappear and chaos and revolution will be inevitable. Lipton herself concedes that the present ratio of white to black per capita income of 10.9 to 1 is "morally indefensible and socially explosive." But her conclusion that because previous predictions of revolution have proved wrong, current predictions are also probably wrong is specious reasoning. The present situation must be examined in its own light, and the evidence is compelling that token changes that might have been acceptable before are no longer acceptable now. If they are offered, they will not satisfy black demands or defuse the explosive tensions.

This is particularly evident when considering the role of Western firms in South Africa. As Lipton points out, the performance of many British companies to date has been far from impressive; instead of stretching the limits of the apartheid system by vigorously promoting black economic interests, many firms have been more than happy to accept the premises of the South African system in pursuit of quick profits. They have made segregation and discrimination regular features of their operations, and they have refused to negotiate with black trade unions.

U.S. corporations have a somewhat better record when it comes to phasing out segregation and discrimination. The recent "statement of principle" by twelve major U.S. firms involved in South Africa spells out a commitment to providing "equal pay for equal work" and elimination of segregated facilities. But the statement says nothing about the central issue of recognizing black unions. "Many of the problems which the manifesto seeks to tackle arise in large part from the fact that Africans are denied collective bargaining rights," asserted the *Financial Mail*. Both black employees and white employers have pointed out that such a general statement of principle is likely to have little if any immediate impact, and the praise the statement drew from the South African government itself has raised suspicions that the prime motive for the statement might be simply to dissuade the Carter administration from supporting a withdrawal of American investment from South Africa.

Aside from the faulty assumption that adequate time

remains for a drawn-out evolutionary process to work, the most glaring weakness of option 2 is that it is now rejected by a growing number of blacks within South Africa. Even a relative moderate like Gatsha Buthelezi has entertained the idea of sanctions. "If economic sanctions can be used to avoid bloodshed and South Africans killing each other, I'll be for them," the Zulu chieftain has declared.[2] Black leaders do not deny that a withdrawal of Western funds will hurt many blacks economically, but they argue that short-term sacrifices must be made to achieve a meaningful political solution. Since the Vorster regime clearly has no intention of initiating any fundamental changes of its own accord, both internal and external pressures must be applied. Internal pressures in the form of black protests are sure to continue; the question for the United States is whether it will heed the call of black leaders for the application of external pressures—in other words, option 3.

At the moment, the Carter administration appears to be formulating its policy on that issue. For the reasons outlined above—especially the sense that the time left for finding a peaceful solution in South Africa is running out—option 2 is no longer considered a realistic response to the situation. "I wouldn't go on the basis of Carter's pre-election *Financial Times* interview," says one U.S. official involved in the South Africa debate. "It no longer means anything."

That does not signal a decision by the administration to go with option 3—the imposition of economic and political sanctions against South Africa. "There's a long way between doing nothing and going to the extremes of imposing immediate sanctions," says the U.S. official. However, some modified version of option 3 appears to be under serious consideration, and I would contend that this is precisely the type of policy

[206]

that should be adopted as a response to the current situation.

The arguments against sanctions are well-known: aside from hurting black workers, sanctions would deprive the West of a major source of raw materials and an important trade outlet. In addition, as the Rhodesian example appeared to prove, sanctions are almost impossible to enforce, and widespread violations can be expected even by the most vociferous enemies of the white regime. The net psychological result will be that the Afrikaners will simply feel more embattled than ever before, reinforcing their determination not to give any concessions to the blacks for fear that once they give in on anything they will be faced with the give-them-an-inch-they'll-take-a-mile syndrome.

The sanctions debate has often started with the mistaken premise that the imposition of sanctions would be a one-stroke operation that would represent a total turnaround in U.S. policy. In looking at the extensive Western involvement in South Africa outlined above, it is readily apparent that this would not be the case. A political decision to impose sanctions would of necessity have to be implemented gradually. Alternate sources of minerals provided by South Africa could not be developed overnight; the existing U.S. business interests in South Africa could not simply pack up and leave on a moment's notice, and most trade deals already contracted for would have to be fulfilled. Therefore, the sanctions option is inherently more flexible and more complex than is generally perceived.

The Rhodesian parallel is both instructive and misleading. Instructive because it does point out the folly of assuming that international resolutions on sanctions can by themselves bring a country with considerable economic resources to its knees; as long as there's a healthy profit to be made by sanctions-

[207]

busters, sanctions-busting will be practiced by operators from countries of every conceivable ideological stripe. Misleading because there are marked differences in the Rhodesian and South African situations and because the fact that sanctions did not work as planned in Rhodesia does not necessarily mean they would not have some impact on South Africa.

In Rhodesia's case, a relatively small, prosperous nation was officially condemned by the United Nations, but its largest, most powerful neighbor offered the Smith regime its full support. South Africa could easily make up for a large part of the trade that was curtailed between Rhodesia and other countries, and it also provided an open channel for sanctions-busters. Given South Africa's wealth and its vast coastline, both the temptation and the means for sanctions-busting exist should sanctions be imposed. However, the very size of South Africa's economy makes it in some ways more vulnerable than Rhodesia; its need for trade and investment are of a much larger magnitude. With the South African economy already seriously strained by a large balance-of-payments deficit and the sudden slowdown of new investment after the Soweto violence, an even partially successful move by the West to cut back its trade and investment would create very serious problems for South Africa. At the moment, 56 percent of the South African economy depends on trade, 75 percent of which is with the West.

The initiative for any such move would have to come from Washington. Britain is too deeply involved in South Africa already; and based on past performance, there is no reason to believe that France or West Germany would seek to lead a crusade that sacrifices short-range economic advantages for long-term political and moral objectives. But that does not mean that the United States would necessarily be the only

[208]

major Western nation to impose sanctions; a decision by the Carter administration to announce publicly and then gradually impose some form of sanctions would in itself put considerable pressure on its allies to follow suit. A nation like France, which has major trade links with black Africa, would be placed in the increasingly awkward position of not going along with a U.S.-Third World initiative on South Africa.

The United States could consider a wide variety of economic and political sanctions. As a first step, the Carter administration could clearly signal its resolve to move toward option 3 by taking a number of unilateral measures aimed at cutting off any official ties between the two countries that could be interpreted as supportive of South Africa. For instance, all nuclear power-sharing agreements could be abrogated, the U.S. Embassy in Pretoria could be downgraded by the withdrawal of U.S. military attachés and some other personnel, and all communications links and intelligence cooperation could be severed. On the business side, EXIM bank loan guarantees could be withdrawn, and the government could stress the risk element to U.S. bankers who continue their involvement in South Africa. The administration could also first attempt to dissuade investors from putting new money into South Africa and as a next step tighten tax credits for companies doing business there. With that as a starting point, the United States could move toward broader initiatives. There is even the possibility that the United States could exert enough pressure on Iran and the oil multinationals to cut off South Africa's oil supplies.

The purpose of any such measures would be to convince South Africans that they really do stand alone, that they cannot expect the West to continue its de facto support of South Africa, or even that the West will remain neutral as

[209]

long as the government remains intransigent in its opposition to black demands for a transformation of the political system. A confrontation within South Africa between black demands and white intransigence is inevitable, and it can be argued that by applying new pressures the United States may be pushing the date of that confrontation forward. But the later such a confrontation takes place, the more likely it is to be uncontrollably violent, with both sides taking such diametrically opposite positions that no reconciliation will be possible. Consequently, the only hope for the United States to play a positive role in South Africa is to force the whites there to face up to the need for a change before it is too late.

As the United States gradually applies sanctions, the South Africans will have time to respond if they choose to; they will not be able to claim they did not know what was coming. And any signs that such a response is forthcoming could be followed by a reverse process: a gradual easing of sanctions as long as the positive response continues. The United States should remain open to such a possibility and make that clear to the South Africans themselves.

There is no guarantee option 3 will really produce the desired result: an agreement by white South Africans to scrap apartheid and grant blacks the political power-sharing they demand. A more important factor will inevitably be the internal pressures brought to bear by the black population. But the United States must attempt to play a positive role, reinforcing those pressures and taking an unambiguous stand that will shatter all remaining white South African illusions. For our part, we must have no illusions of our own that sanctions by themselves will force white South Africa to see reason, but they may just help. True, they may not—it could already be too late to avert the "smash-up." But by doing anything less, the United States would make a bloody racial confrontation in South Africa not only probable but inevitable.

NOTES

1. Merle Lipton, "British Investment in South Africa: Is Constructive Engagement Possible?" *South African Labour Bulletin,* October 1976.

2. Interview with the author, *Newsweek International,* May 23, 1977.

[211]

[SEVEN]

U.S. Policy Toward Africa

Jennifer Seymour Whitaker

In the aftermath of Henry Kissinger's episodic diplomacy, the Carter administration began to seek a restrained grand design to shape its increasing involvement with Africa. As enunciated by Secretary of State Cyrus Vance six months into the new administration, the emerging Africa policy emphasized the need to take an affirmative rather than a reactive approach, minimize the East-West competition so as not to allow it to distort regional events, recognize the importance to African states of economic development and indigenous nationalism, and affirm that economic cooperation and active diplomacy will constitute the main forms of interaction, with military ties and arms sales downplayed.[1]

Apart from the pressing issues in southern Africa, the outlines of this policy could provide a blueprint for a U.S. approach to the Third World as a whole. Both for Africa and for the Third World generally it is an eminently sensible policy, rationally designed to utilize U.S. political and eco-

[212]

nomic opportunities and, even more important, to avoid the political and military traps inherent in approaches emphasizing the U.S.-Soviet competition.

Implicit in the grand strategy is the painful main lesson of Vietnam—beware of entangling involvement in Third World military conflicts. Thus the United States seeks to de-emphasize the short-term military aspects of the competition with the Soviets and focus instead on a longer-term assertion of U.S. initiatives for political and economic cooperation with African states.

However, the military competition unfortunately continues to dominate not only our own but also most of the rest of the world's perceptions of the United States and the Soviet Union. The superpowers' military score-cards are deeply ingrained in international sensibilities. With the United States immobilized in, and then pulling back from, Vietnam, while the U.S.S.R. was pouring resources into the expansion of its navy and strategic power, the latter came to be viewed as a power on the move, while the former was contracting. The success of the Soviet-Cuban intervention in Angola confirmed this impression, engendering fear in our European allies, renewed zeal in the Soviets, some skepticism among Africans about the old power of the United States versus the new vigor of the U.S.S.R., and self-doubt (publicly manifested by the Secretary of State) in Americans. These feelings about the national will play a part as real as guns (or butter) in foreign-policy decision-making.

Furthermore, most of the recent Soviet assertive actions in Africa have been responses to opportunities presented by regional crises in which the Soviet Union could assume the role of military patron to clients of widely varying degrees of ideological affinity. Opportunities for military patronage are likely to occur frequently throughout the continent, which

[213]

appears destined for a period of extended upheaval, but particularly in southern Africa.

Thus, despite all good, carefully formulated intentions, Africa's crises and Soviet opportunism therein will continue to confront the United States with immediate choices about military involvement. The difficulties in avoiding a reactive policy—an African version of containment [2]—became evident less than a month after Vance's enunciation of sweet reason. In an abrupt turnabout, the State Department announced on July 27 that the United States would supply arms "to the African region" to "challenge the Soviet Union in a strategically important part of the world" and thereby avoid giving the impression that it was passively watching the Russians make inroads there, as well as to show African countries "that if they break with the Russians they can count on help from the United States." [3]

In this announcement of proffered U.S. aid to Somalia, Chad, and the Sudan, the vulnerability of the long-term design to distortion by immediate choices was manifest. Subsequently, growing U.S. concern about Soviet-Cuban military initiatives—and the appearance of U.S. inaction—in the Horn and Zaire made further inroads into the resolve to avoid a reactive policy. Hence, the potential contradictions between the longer-range policy and day-to-day decision-making, particularly regarding the military aspects of various regional power struggles: How can we vigorously maintain our side of the U.S.-Soviet competition while eschewing alliances based on anticommunism? How can we play an active role vis-à-vis Africa while curtailing our military involvement there? Does the long-term policy arise out of wishful "do-goodism"—and perhaps a reflexive reaction to our Vietnam experience—or is it based on a realistic calculus of our own capabilities and the locale in which we are deploying them?

In Vietnam the United States attempted to "contain communism" in the most direct way possible—by deployment of American soldiers in a Third World conflict. As Sino-Soviet hostility has intensified, our perception of international communism's threat to our own security has changed. However, Vietnam altered our view of ourselves in relation to the rest of the world in a perhaps more profound way. Most Americans now view the prospect of sending U.S. troops to fight almost anywhere outside this country as utterly foolish.

During nearly a decade of warfare in that Third World country, we learned the contemporary perils of interposing ourselves in a local civil conflict and of trying to resist the tides of indigenous nationalism. With our focus on the place of Vietnam in the East-West power balance, we failed to pay due attention to the local forces in play and often failed to read them accurately. The will and the ways of the Vietnamese combatants, not the designs of the other great powers, caused our downfall. The Angolan debacle, which followed directly on the heels of our ouster from Vietnam, again underlined the traps inherent in a strategy based on reaction to Soviet initiatives rather than on an assessment of local forces.

These insights are evidently basic to Secretary Vance's general approach to U.S. relationships with Africa, as enunciated in July 1977. To the extent that they reflect profound changes in the international environment resulting from the new sovereign statehood of numerous poor and often unstable former colonies, they are also fundamental to our stance vis-à-vis involvements in other parts of the Third World.

In Latin America, Asia, and the Middle East, as well as in Africa, the United States today finds itself dealing with an array of nations whose collective (not necessarily concerted) political impact cannot be estimated by traditional measures. With the end of the colonial era and the approximate military

[215]

strategic balance between East and West, the powerful can less easily control weaker client states. Neither superpower can enforce its policies toward Third World nations by military power. In addition, a conscious rejection of dependency—particularly in economic relations with the industrialized nations—has become a prime ingredient in the nationalism which animates the political life of the former colonies. Finally, the Third World countries have undertaken collective efforts to improve their leverage with industrialized nations.

The new enormous wealth and consequent influence of the oil-producing nations are both a primary cause and a reflection of the diffusion of authority. The oil producers' growing economic power in relation to the OECD countries has created a new sort of triangular relationship. The action of the OPEC nations in escalating the price of oil also pushed economic issues into the international political spotlight for both the OECD countries and the Third World.

Anomalously, while the Soviet Union may reap some political benefits from the dominance in North-South discourse of calls for "equity" and "redistribution," its irrelevance to the economic development of most of the Third World excludes it quite completely from this primary arena of influence. For example, the U.S.S.R. was not present in the main arena of economic bargaining on issues of resources, trade, debt, commodities during 1976 and 1977—that is, the Paris Conference on International Economic Cooperation (CIEC). Thus both superpowers face a world in which commitments are likely to prove ephemeral, and the correspondence between ideology and national interest is blurred and shifting. In such an environment, it would seem wisest for the United States to base its policy on a tolerance for diversity akin to the pluralism that is central to our own political system.

Not merely a hopeful humanitarianism—or a temporary

[216]

failure of nerve—but also a considered judgment of our recent experience and of the changing international environment, then, inform the nonbellicose, meliorative, *long-term* approach of Secretary Vance's policy statement. It must be acknowledged, however, that the formulation of the long-term policy was given impetus by the pressure of immediate crises. The possibility that the Russians would gain advantage from impending conflicts throughout the continent and particularly from racial strife in southern Africa first focused the minds of U.S. policy makers. In a sense, then, the enunciated determination *not* to respond to African events in cold-war terms flowed from a policy review sparked by a potential U.S.-Soviet competition in Africa.

We cannot ignore the potential for a military competition in Africa. Nor can we limit our own political leverage by foreswearing all military involvement there. But in order to avoid a defensive posture, we must base our policy on several imperatives which spring from the situation we now face. Southern Africa must receive primary emphasis because of its particular dangers and because it is in many ways the key to U.S. relations with all of Africa. The basic components of our strategy, however, apply to our stance vis-à-vis the continent as a whole. First, we should ground our policy firmly in an understanding of African realities and focus primarily on opportunities and traps which await us there rather than on Soviet advances and retreats. Second, as far as possible, we should maneuver to keep U.S.-Soviet competition located in spheres other than the military. Third, we should put forward our own view of a more desirable future world and show the will to achieve it. Finally, we should go on the offensive in "selling" our positive Africa policy.

How do these ground rules apply to the pursuit of particular U.S. interests and the achievement of general U.S. goals in

[217]

Africa? As Gordon Bertolin indicates in Chapter 1, the current U.S. economic stake in Africa is relatively small although significant, particularly in the case of Nigerian oil. Strategic interests center first on the security of the Cape route for transporting U.S. and European oil imports, and secondarily on access to Nigerian oil and southern African minerals. Primary political interests include African cooperation with U.S. aims in the Middle East and the achievement of an orderly transition to just power-sharing in southern Africa. The overall goal of U.S. policy in Africa is to protect these interests and at the same time advance more general international aims as they are affected by African issues.

These broader concerns include: cooperative multilateral political relationships in a world where "conference diplomacy" is on the rise, as for instance at the United Nations, where the Africans comprise a third of the membership; openness to the United States—chiefly with regard to economic access, but also diplomatic discourse and media coverage; receptivity to basic tenets of human rights; the peaceful settlement of disputes. In addition, certain basic physical problems lay claim to universal concern: hunger; ecological depredation, as in the advance of the Sahara; burgeoning population growth. Finally, African "development" progress is more an African than a U.S. interest, but it can be a means to other U.S. ends, as well as an object of humanitarian concern itself. Although we cannot depend on economic and political development to moderate violent conflict in the short term—in fact, it may have the opposite effect—it is even less likely that continued unremitting poverty and disorganization will produce stability.

Obviously, these general goals offer such a broad field for endeavor that they could swallow an almost infinite amount of U.S. energy and resources, whereas the means at our disposal for effecting our Africa policy are limited. However, the most crucial U.S. political and strategic interests in Africa and to some extent also our world order goals coalesce for the short term in our concern for a peaceful transition to majority rule in Rhodesia, Namibia, and South Africa. With respect to our primary economic interests and goals, maintaining good relations with Nigeria would seem to come first; then, a peaceful transition to majority rule in southern Africa is also crucial, particularly as regards the heavy South African investment of our ally Britain. More broadly, multilateral economic cooperation (as with the rest of the Third World) involves both political and economic interests. The latter will be served to the extent that the ongoing New International Economic Order (NIEO) negotiations may result in the sort of open environment that has in this century seemed best for the U.S. economy. We may also hope that NIEO reforms will further economic development.

Understanding African Realities

Most of our multilateral and bilateral interests in Africa exist independently of the East-West tug-of-war. The concrete African political and economic realities which should instead underlie U.S. policy choices have been analyzed in some detail elsewhere in this book, particularly in Chapters 1, 3 and 6. Several broader factors, however, will be emphasized here: the role of African nationalism and the significance of current leftward trends.

For the superpowers' (or any outside power's) relationships in Africa and much of the Third World, an understanding of two aspects of African nationalism is crucial: first, the importance of sovereignty, or independence of external control, to Third World leadership; and second, the central role of various forms of nationalism in consolidating or obstructing internal control. The word "nationalism," in fact, expresses both the *state's* drive for control (vis-à-vis the outside world) and the jockeying for control of various ethnic groups within the state. In combination with other closely related factors—leadership, resources, external relationships—it determines how the plant will grow, how the nation-state will develop.

In Africa, the fragility of the new states' sovereignty and the extreme volatility of many competing nationalisms has intensified the significance of these forces. Consciousness of their vulnerability impelled the African nations to codify their sovereignty and national independence in the Charter of the Organization of African Unity (OAU): first, in prohibiting the alteration of their colonial borders, and, second, in condemning external intervention in African affairs. While both prohibitions have been somewhat weakened by recent events, the protean character of African political development as well as the value placed on national independence bode ill for would-be patron-client relationships. Thus the workings of African nationalism dictate a flexible strategy on the part of outside powers.

Likewise, an analysis of development trends also indicates the importance of a pluralistic approach. For various reasons, a discernible leftward trend in internal African political and economic structures will probably continue for some time to come. Widespread poverty lends moral suasion to egalitarian ideologies, and the fragility of political systems makes firm authoritarian control almost inevitably appealing. Given the paucity of material resources, ideology is required as a mobilizing force, and Marxism is most conveniently at hand. The results of African socialist experimentation may not bear much resemblance to either the Soviet or the Chinese model—

[220]

in fact, Cuba or Mozambique may often be more attractive models—but Marxism will provide a dominant ideology and rhetoric.

How far this will go remains to be seen. The very poverty and lack of structure (or of personnel to man an extensive bureaucracy) militate against successful socialist government except where massive external aid is available to fill the breach. The current elites of ·the wealthiest African countries (Nigeria, Ivory Coast, Gabon, Kenya, Zambia, and Zaire) would resist a redistributive or leveling strategy. Nonetheless, the public sector of most African economies at present controls a large proportion of national resources, and this trend seems unlikely to be reversed. For the younger educated class, socialism gets a significant boost from the taint of the Western (colonial) antecedents hanging about the idea of "capitalism." In this regard, a move to the left may in part constitute a quest for national independence—to the extent that socialism represents the casting off of cultural and economic dependency on the West—and African takeovers of Western investment are its concrete manifestation.

Toward this trend the United States should so far as possible remain neutral. The development of democratic political systems in Africa should *not* be a goal of U.S. policy. Although such a result would be immensely gratifying to us, it is, first of all, well beyond our power to influence, except in terms of our example. Second, evolution within African countries toward the civic mind-set required for national democratic government will take time where it occurs at all. Again it should be explicitly stated that the formation of capitalist economic systems should *not* be a U.S. goal. While we do considerably affect the shape of African economies, mainly through our investment, it is not at all clear that a Western economic model would be appropriate to many African countries. Nor is

[221]

any particular development model clearly (a) best for African countries or (b) best for the United States.

Almost two decades of African independence is far too short a period for reliable generalizations about the significance of various patterns of African development. Therefore an obvious—and again, obviously transitory—factor must bear a significant amount of weight in our calculus of the viability of states: that is the quality of their leaderships, and particularly their ability to hold a nation together. Among the alternative forms of political and economic development (crudely termed "socialist" or "capitalist") for the new African states, we find states doing more or less "well" or "badly" by several measures: use of the country's natural resources to fulfill the needs of its population and lay the basis for future growth, development of the country's human resources, and the degree and extent of popular economic and political participation. Maintaining national order is a precondition for gains in these areas; and an increase in national cohesion may be an effect.

The commitment and intelligence of national leaders in pursuing these goals are basic to their achievement. An assessment of both commitment and effectiveness should inform U.S. economic aid allocations. Furthermore, progress in these areas may over the longer term increase the "stability" of the state, and thereby underpin political relations somewhat more firmly.

Divisive internal nationalism and problematical leadership have come together in two putative clients of the superpowers, Zaire and Ethiopia. In both states these forces make the role of military patron precarious. When former U.S. Secretary of Defense Donald Rumsfeld made a démarche to sell arms to Zaire in 1976, apparently out of concern for threats to Zaire by left-wing neighbors, he seemingly ignored the question whether the greater threat to Zaire was not that of internal dissolution. The Soviets also seem to have disregarded the question of viability in their commitment to Ethiopia in 1977. Had they looked harder at the violent internecine conflicts in the Ethiopian leadership, the quantity of internal irredentisms, and of course the intractibility of Somali national claims on Ethiopia's Ogaden, would they have leapt at the opportunity? Probably. They are beginning to be capable of the sorts of Third World interventions the United States was able to indulge in for many years with relative impunity. And the role of military patron to Ethiopia's leftist revolution would appear to have an irresistible attraction. In any case, in consequence of the all-important local questions of nationalism and leadership, they now find themselves deeply involved in dilemmas that are likely to be both expensive and impervious to their manipulation.

It is important to recognize these forces in assessing Soviet activity in Africa. Somali nationalism, directed against Ethiopia, caused the summary end to all strategic payoff from the Soviet Union's extensive military aid to Somalia. The Somali action illustrates well the futility of efforts to create military clients. Ethiopia will undoubtedly cost the Soviets much more in both material and political terms. In Eritrea, the Ethiopian army had, by late 1977, well-nigh lost the struggle with the Eritrean insurgents, and to revive the Ethiopian cause might require pitting Cuban personnel against dug-in and highly motivated guerrilla fighters. In addition, the heavy build-up of Cuban troops and the reported use of Soviet soldiers in the Ogaden against the U.S.S.R.'s former ally, Somalia, raised the specter of a new—Soviet—imperialism that could become an increasing liability for the Russians over the long haul. Finally, given the extreme instability of the Dergue, the U.S.S.R.'s Ethiopian investment could prove no more lasting than its Somali venture.

[223]

U.S. efforts to influence the direction of internal African political development through support of moderates or hostility (subversion?) toward radicals are, for the reasons noted above, likely to be even less successful. That is, in blindly supporting relatively conservative "pro-West" regimes, we would frequently find ourselves supporting an uncertain status quo. We wisely sidestepped this pitfall in Zaire in the Shaba crisis in March 1977, though not so easily in May 1978. Ultimately, of course, the two revolutions which the Soviets have taken under their wing—Angola and Ethiopia—present the same problem: the "revolutionaries" become the status quo which may ultimately have to be protected against competing nationalist forces.

In southern Africa, an ability to work with regimes of all political colorations has already been the key to our diplomatic efforts. The white regimes may be considered anti-Communist bastions. They have expected (and may still hope) that the presence of the U.S.S.R. on the side of their enemies would insure Western support against these foes. Yet the effectiveness of U.S. diplomacy has depended on an ability to deal as well with the southern African front-line states. These have included the "moderates," Zambia and Botswana; "socialist" Tanzania; and Soviet-Cuban (and Chinese) aided "radicals," Angola and Mozambique. The latter are likely to play a continuing key role in determining the character of the Rhodesian and Namibian transitions as long as the guerrilla struggles persist, because the liberationists depend on them for their shelter and support. These countries will also be involved in shaping future military pressures on South Africa. The recent more friendly, forthcoming stance toward the Mozambican regime on the part of the U.S. administration has undoubtedly facilitated diplomatic processes in the area and may be a necessary condition for future success.

Avoiding Superpower Military Competition

In the years of difficult choices on southern Africa that lie ahead for the United States, a pluralistic approach may be increasingly difficult to maintain. Hence the need to emphasize the second imperative: the particular dangers and distortions inherent in a U.S.-Soviet military competition in Africa. The temptations will be many.

Several chapters in this book have emphasized the convergent (and related) trends in Africa that are now increasing the potential incidence of violent conflicts in which outside military aid will be sought. First of all, the consolidation process in the young nation-states will continue to be disrupted by internal jockeying for power—particularly among ethnic groups—as is predicted, for example, in Kenya after Kenyatta. Second, the plethora of military governments throughout the continent indicates that coups may well be a frequent mode for transferring power. Third, although Africa's borders have seemed until now relatively fixed, the initially successful Somali incursions into Ethiopia's Ogaden region presage ethnic irredentism, resulting in military pressure on the borders (and territory) of such states as Ghana, Chad, the Sudan, Kenya, Zaire and Angola. Fourth, internal disorder may be projected into regional clashes, as in the current case of Uganda. Fifth, more than in the past, the ideological differences of neighboring states may result in conflict, as in the political strife between "capitalist" Kenya and "socialist" Tanzania. And the increase in Soviet- and Western-sponsored arms races between hostile neighbors spurs the growth of mutual fears and encourages the development of military reflexes. The potential for this sort of future conflict exists between Kenya and Uganda, Kenya and

[225]

Somalia, Zaire and either Angola or Congo, the Sudan and Ethiopia, Zambia and either Angola or Mozambique.

For various reasons, some of which have already been discussed, strategic and political competition in Africa may appear relatively attractive to the Soviet Union over the next decade or two. As Robert Legvold argues, the Soviet Union "from the perspective of politics . . . finds more encouragement" in Africa than any other part of the Third World today. As we have seen, a significant leftward pull exists, generating at least temporary affinities with the U.S.S.R.

More important, the ability of the Russians to offer direct military assistance to the southern African liberation movements has provided the U.S.S.R. with a steady source of political capital and potential military ties with the incoming regimes in areas liberated by guerrilla warfare. The Soviet Union will continue to be presented with this sort of opportunity while the transition to majority rule is in process. As far as African politics is concerned, aid to liberation struggles in southern Africa has been regarded in a distinct—and unimpeachable—category. Though a front-line state like Zambia would very likely prefer that the new Zimbabwe regime (after a transition to majority rule) not come into being with close links to the U.S.S.R., Zambia's president, Kenneth Kaunda, would be the first to declare that any aid in the liberation struggle, no matter what the source, answers the deepest needs of all Africans. Internal political settlements—i.e., excluding the guerrillas—in Rhodesia or Namibia would of course alter this calculus. The black-white struggle in South Africa itself, however, offers a field of protracted opportunity. Inhibitions on U.S. military aid to the guerrillas are unlikely to dissolve. Nor should they. We would find it impossible to pursue political avenues toward a "peaceful" settlement while

[226]

simultaneously fostering a military resolution. Thus in southern Africa the United States is stuck in a posture of rhetorical support for the *cause* of the liberation movements that cannot be buttressed by military aid. Widespread guerrilla struggle in the area could work to Soviet advantage in several ways: by sharpening racial antagonisms and thus swelling anti-Western biases on the part of the incoming leaders; by hastening the breakdown of Western (capitalist) economic structures in the three countries; by increasing the influence of the guerrilla fighters (presumed "radicalized" and dependent on Soviet aid) in the incoming regimes.

Soviet military aid outside of southern Africa does not of course enjoy the same widespread political approbation. In fact, African states threatened by Soviet-armed neighbors have begun to express rising concern about the increasing Soviet military role (and the presence of Cuban troops). Some of these states sponsored a resolution directed against Soviet intervention at the OAU meeting in Libreville in July 1977.[4]

However, even outside southern Africa the U.S.S.R. is likely to emphasize military means in both increasing its influence with individual African nations and improving its overall power position vis-à-vis the United States. It is, quite obviously, better equipped in this sphere than in the economic or diplomatic areas. Lacking the leverage afforded by overseas investment and a large volume of trade, the Soviet Union has also chosen to allocate only minimal resources to economic aid. Nor in the strictest sense would its ideology allow it to dole out aid, in the Western fashion, to prop up regimes that should be ripe for revolution. Diplomatically, the U.S.S.R. has not been notably successful in its African relationships. In the southern African conflict (as in the Middle East) it is not placed to play a political role like that recently tried by the

[227]

United States. So it will play from its best suit, one in which its own advantages are sometimes reinforced by U.S. disadvantages.

The military elements in a superpower competition for influence range from "showing the flag" by their respective navies, arms sales, training, grant military aid, military advisers, various levels of basing agreements, to airlifting of materiel during a conflict, air support during a conflict and, finally, troop support. While the initial military ties, particularly arms sales, may be politically noncontroversial, they are often the first phase of a developing pattern of commitments.

The United States still outdistances the Soviet Union in actual military capability to "project force" in the Third World. This superiority is offset, however, as has already been noted, by significant political curbs on the use of the U.S. capability. The United States has much less freedom for maneuver than does the U.S.S.R. in this sort of competition; in the aftermath of Vietnam, the obstructive power likely to be wielded by Congress and the press regarding entangling commitments in the Third World is considerable. If this resistance does not deter the administration from offering commitments, it may nevertheless engender considerable skepticism on the part of prospective recipients. Neither fancy footwork (as in the Soviet airlift of Cuban troops to Angola) nor significant long-term commitments outside the European arena (which includes Israel and Japan) seems possible in terms of U.S. domestic politics: as for the former, secrecy would probably be short-lived in such an operation; while the credibility of the latter is obviously called into question in view of the strong possibility that succeeding administrations will alter the politics of their predecessors.

If the terms of a military competition in Africa would seem

to favor the U.S.S.R., the actual strategic problems that Soviet activity in Africa may pose for the United States do not seem very threatening. As Geoffrey Kemp's analysis in Chapter 4 indicates, hostile black states around the southern African littoral would occasion increased insecurity in a crisis situation but represent no real threat in wartime.[5] Regarding access to strategic resources, it seems unlikely that the emerging black regimes of southern Africa would find it in their own national interest to withhold their minerals from Western industrial nations, which constitute the world market. While "Soviet-controlled" regimes in either the Indian Ocean region or southern Africa would constitute a greater danger to wartime logistics, ways of compensating for the loss of the Cape route and the U.S.S.R.'s vulnerabilities along its own littoral would soon erase the Soviet advantage. Likewise, as Andrew Nagorski argues in Chapter 6, a complete closing of the Cape route to oil tankers could only be effected by the Soviet Union, and it would inevitably be part of a much larger conflict in which emergency stockpiles of oil and other minerals would automatically be called into play.

Thus the gravest threat in Russian military activity in Africa is probably perceptual—in the fears, doubts, hopes that Soviet military aid and acquisition of basing rights may create about shifts in the U.S.-Soviet balance of power. This must be taken seriously. But in the choices that may be forced upon the United States by African upheavals and Soviet activism, an old-style containment presents particularly inappropriate guidelines.

Crises force choices. The extent to which freedom of choice is limited in a crisis, however, depends upon decisions taken beforehand. Even seemingly trivial decisions may lead to U.S. commitments which will foreclose future options. Numerous African conflicts will, of course, continue to arise and subside

[229]

without attracting any serious external attention whatsoever. With the variety of situations facing the United States in Africa, however, all military involvement cannot be precluded. Thus it is necessary to examine ways in which tactics for minimalist military interaction might be applied. Underlying this discussion are several assumptions. First, for reasons discussed previously, preventive and nonmilitary means will be consistently preferred and applied to maintain U.S. influence and preserve U.S. interests. Second, in order to guard this resolve, negative injunctions about military involvement should have priority in contingency planning. The United States should *not,* as a matter of predetermined policy: deploy U.S. troops in African conflicts; enter into military alliances or basing arrangements in Africa; play a major role in the arms trade in the region.

At this historical juncture, executive or Congressional endorsement for direct U.S. military involvement in an African conflict—meaning air or naval support as well as participation of U.S. troops—seems out of the question. (It should not be forgotten, however, that a swift change of public attitudes is also characteristic of this era.) Beyond that seemingly extreme contingency, the relatively low level of U.S. national interests and the protean character of African politics render military alliances an unnecessary and highly uncertain proposition.

Like military alliances, basing arrangements, or the acquisition of facilities, will probably be tempting chiefly to the extent that the Soviets are acquiring them. But political trends have shorn the United States of many overseas bases in recent years, and it has readily adjusted to the new situation. American naval technologies permit long-distance cruising as the Russians' do not. Moreover, in the putative competition for facilities, Soviet gains have not been overwhelming. Only

Somalia accorded the Soviet Union basing rights—now summarily withdrawn. And as the game of musical chairs in the Horn has shown, the strategic gains to either superpower in a would-be patron-client relationship in Africa are likely to be ephemeral.

As I. William Zartman and Geoffrey Kemp point out, arms sales and military aid raise more difficult questions. When African regimes wish to buy arms from us or request military aid, the presumption should be, as previously argued, that our assent will be infrequent and reluctant. The Carter administration has heavily emphasized its reservations about arms sales for several convincing reasons: (1) to avoid automatic U.S. involvement in local conflicts; (2) to discourage local arms races which may increase the likelihood of conflict; and (3) to minimize the diversion of scarce resources into arms. Yet this policy is proving exceedingly difficult to implement. Eschewing arms sales not only creates frictions with nations which may be important to the United States (like the Middle East oil powers) but also means giving up one of the relatively few deployable means of influence available to U.S. officials.

Nonetheless, it should be emphasized that arms sales and military aid carry with them a structure of commitments—in a way that economic projects do not—in that the *use* of U.S.-made weapons generates a virtually automatic need for more ammunition, spare parts, and replacement weapons. Further, their use in war generates a need to which the United States is constrained to *respond.* We were caught in this sort of trap in Ethiopia through 1975, and would have found real difficulty in extricating ourselves had not that country's new military regime fortuitously turned to the extreme left. Our response may be positive or negative, but either way we are then involved in the crisis, whether or not we wish to be. Political decisions about resupply may put us in the position of

[231]

adjudicating African quarrels whose elements may not even be wholly clear to us. They may also raise questions about our reliability, or the degree to which we "honor our commitments" (in comparison with the Soviet Union).

In responding to specific requests, a number of criteria should be examined. Is the country significant in terms of U.S. interests; is its government relatively viable; does the state in question need arms or military aid to counter an external threat; and, emphatically, are not alternative arms suppliers available among Western countries or their allies? The gravest perceptual threat to U.S. interests would arise from Soviet involvement in the subversion of regimes having significant political or economic importance to Western countries.[6] But subversion should be clearly distinguished from Soviet military aid to existing regimes, as in Ethiopia. Aside from southern Africa, military aid is the U.S.S.R.'s main mode of present activity and is likely to remain so. Internal disorder or dissidence, though it may give rise to serious insecurities for the existing regime, should not call forth U.S. arms sales or military aid.

Most African countries, under most circumstances, would be excluded according to these criteria. Only Nigeria is of sufficient economic and political significance to the United States to warrant arms sales as part of a pattern of developing political cooperation.

Somalia presents a well-nigh perfect test case of U.S. resolve not to conduct its policy in Africa by outbidding the Soviets. Somalia's army was designed for aggression against its neighbors and was used very effectively to gain control of Ethiopia's Ogaden. But with the Soviet Union now aiding Ethiopia, pressure is being put on the United States to help the now bitterly anti-Soviet Somalia. In March 1977, the Assistant

Secretary of State for African Affairs journeyed to Mogadishu to discuss U.S. supply of "defensive weapons" to Somalia. Weapons actually needed for defense might be supplied; but despite the urging of Iran, Saudi Arabia, and other Arab allies of Somalia, the United States should not provide Somalia with arms which could be used to threaten Ethiopia once again—or Kenya. Instead, it should maintain diplomatic ties and economic aid relations with both regimes and strive for cooperative peace-making with the Soviet Union.

Nor should the United States supply "counterinsurgency" aircraft to Morocco in its conflict with the Polisario guerrillas of the Sahara. Washington should, instead, maintain official neutrality between the two sets of participants in the conflict— Morocco and Mauritania, Algeria and the Polisario—and support a U.N. plebiscite in which the territory's inhabitants could exercise self-determination regarding their future.

In the future, Zimbabwe is likely to present the United States with numerous choices regarding military assistance—to most of which the response should be negative. The range of possible scenarios for a transition in that country is extensive, but each contains considerable potential for civil conflict. In a settlement supervised by the United Nations, the U.N. peace-keeping force would bear responsibility for transitional security and for creating a Zimbabwean army. On the other hand, a settlement arrived at internally, which does not include the liberation fighters but does, in the view of the front-line states, represent a genuine turnover to majority control, should blunt the motivation of the front-line states to continue supporting the guerrilla war; and opportunities for external subversion would be greatly curtailed and probably within the ability of the new regime to deal with. However, in the event of an internal settlement considered by the front-line states to be a façade for continued white control, U.S. or Western military aid to counter continued insurgency would end all possibilities for effective political cooperation in achieving a peaceful solution in southern Africa. Only if a Zimbabwean regime generally considered in Africa to be "legitimate" were seriously threatened by external subversion, should the United States consider military aid. But it would be better to let the British handle it.

Finally, Zaire has provided the most significant test to date of the basic tenets of U.S. policy. In the Shaba incursion of 1977, we were able to avoid virtually all involvement. In the 1978 repetition, despite an escalation in pugnacious rhetoric, the administration held U.S. actions to a supporting airlift for French and Belgian and then African (Moroccan) troops. For the future, however, the immediate need to shore up this repository of Western loans and investments must not blind us to the risks of becoming embroiled in the conflicts of that shaky and corrupt regime. We should continue to let the French handle active peace-keeping efforts and major arms supplies to Zaire—and support all OAU efforts to protect African borders. Further, we should emphasize political and economic pressures on Zaire—starting with the IMF program—to reform its own house and cut off aid to Angolan insurgents. Finally, we should recognize Angola and use our increased leverage to curtail Angolan and Cuban aid to the Shaba rebels.

Which brings us to a final injunction: the desirability for the United States of letting alternative Western arms suppliers fill even the justified requests for arms or military aid bears reiterating. Thus possible superpower military rivalries may be muted. In addition, the sharing of responsibility among the Western allies increases Western options in a crisis while U.S. military aloofness insures maximum flexibility of response.

[234]

Maintaining U.S. Influence

This assessment of the political uses of military force in Africa has emphasized the negative. The influence we forego in the military sphere, however, should be actively sought through diplomatic and economic means.

With regard to the U.S.S.R. itself, direct and indirect communication with Moscow about conflicting interests in Africa should be determinedly maintained. It goes without saying that where a clash of interests may occur or be threatened, the United States should emphasize its concern to the U.S.S.R., if possible well in advance of a crisis. Apparently, the Soviets were surprised at the intensity of the U.S. reaction to their intervention in Angola; they were not, it would seem, ever directly approached during the covert maneuvering of both sides that preceded the introduction of Cuban troops. Cuban or Soviet aid to a build-up for a bona fide invasion of Zaire or, more hypothetically, of Zambia, would be occasions for urgent bilateral communication. An example of indirect communication is the U.S. slowdown in developing political relations with Cuba, thus signalling U.S. concern for outside military intervention in Africa. That the large Soviet-Cuban presence in Ethiopia threatens broader U.S.-Soviet relations should be signalled urgently in other bilateral negotiations. Over the longer run, efforts to neutralize Africa strategically for both superpowers should also be maintained in the United Nations and through the OAU as well as in direct U.S.-Soviet negotiations like those on the Indian Ocean.

In the diplomatic arena, we will be most effective when we coordinate our efforts with those of key African states. Assiduous diplomatic activity will be required to keep African and U.S. initiatives as closely linked as possible. In crisis-management (and in forestalling the need for it), the active interplay between U.S. and African interests can be used to further both. The basic OAU prohibition against the intervention of outside powers in Africa accords with the U.S. aim of curtailing Soviet military involvement in the continent. Concerted African pressures on the Soviet Union, as in the July 1977 Libreville resolution, are undoubtedly felt by Moscow.

Further, in harmonizing its political and diplomatic initiatives with the flow of African politics, the United States should, as far as possible, coordinate its policies with those of the African nations which influence active intra-African negotiations. Nigeria's size, oil wealth, and huge army make that country an obvious regional leader; now its increasing commitment to the liberation of southern Africa and its funds and support (demonstrated in its donation of $20 million to the Zimbabwean liberation movements in 1977) have brought it expanded political leverage. The economic interdependence between Nigeria and the United States and the Nigerian preference for relatively open economic and political institutions should make close coordination between the two countries obvious and natural. Its possible fruits were exemplified when Nigeria (after discussions with the United States) made its concern felt to the Angolan government about possible Angolan (or Cuban) support for incursions across the Zaire border during the Shaba affair in March 1977.

In southern Africa we have wound our way most successfully through the thicket of liberation politics when we have let ourselves be guided by cooperation with the front-line presidents. The leadership of President Julius Nyerere gives Tanzania, for example, a disproportionate amount of influence on southern African questions within the OAU (and to some extent as well within the front-line states). In the region, the United States will be sought after as a mediator as long as the

[236]

U.S. domestic commitment to a just sharing of power is not at variance with African perceptions of what constitutes the end of white rule and is not outstripped by African demands for various kinds of sanctions against South Africa. Because our influence resides in our ability to deal with both sides, it is crucial that our communications and cooperation with the African leadership not be allowed to break down over the issue of an internal settlement in Rhodesia or Namibia. This would lead to the demise of most of our African initiatives.

For the future, the United Nations will continue to be the main international contact point for many African nations, and U.N. diplomacy is particularly important in African politics. Thus our stepped-up U.N. communication under Ambassador Young and our active diplomatic efforts in southern Africa reinforce each other. In addition, we should multilateralize our southern African diplomacy wherever feasible. To the extent that we can draw on our European allies, our policies toward South Africa will have maximum effect. In the rest of the continent, not only our European allies but now also Arab moderates like Egypt and Saudi Arabia have significant interests. The Egyptians will continue to press within the OAU for condemnations of Soviet "intervention." In the Horn, the Saudi Arabians could use economic leverage to rein further Somali irredentism if they were persuaded this was important to regional peace.

Regarding U.S. economic alternatives within an activist Africa policy, our trade and investment stake in South Africa gives us significant leverage there. The use of economic carrots and sticks to move Pretoria toward sharing power with the country's blacks will be our main means of (a) helping minimize the violence of the transition or (b) at least demonstrating our commitment to power sharing both to Pretoria and the black Africans opposing it.

[237]

As far as aid goes, the direct leverage accrued by aid programs is difficult to measure (the correlation between aid programs and how African countries vote in the United Nations, for example, is indiscernible). The effect is more atmospheric than concrete, with the general levels of a country's aid seen as reflecting the importance the donor attaches to the recipient areas and garnering for it, reciprocally, "influence" there. By this criterion the United States will have to raise its African aid levels considerably from the 1977 level of about 7.5 percent of world totals or $417.3 million, for its economic assistance programs to support in any discernible way its other African initiatives.

The effective allocation of bilateral economic aid necessitates both a method of ordering U.S. priorities and a sometimes closely related ability to respond to African needs.[7] Proposed strategies for choosing (or excluding) aid recipients variously emphasize political, moral or economic criteria, such as supporting U.S. strategic interests; focusing on "important countries"; giving African elites what they want; helping "successful" regimes; rewarding progress in human rights; emphasizing the neediest; giving only to those who make the best use of aid; and focusing on what the United States can do best (e.g., agricultural development). None of these by itself is sufficient, and all should at one time or another be called into play as we monitor African events and our interest therein. The Sudan provides a case in point here. Although the current U.S. interest in the Sudan is undoubtedly heavily influenced by the enmity of that country toward its "radical" Soviet-aligned neighbors (Libya, Ethiopia, Uganda), the growing U.S. economic and political activity there is warranted in local terms by the confluence of a number of these criteria. A sizable and potentially important African country, at present the beneficiary of significant amounts of aid from the oil-producing Arab nations, the Sudan is now moving swiftly to develop its enormous agricultural potential (with the help of the Arabs and the United States). It is to be hoped that the alternatives to military activism in the Sudan will help to contain the enthusiasm for arming this desirable new African "ally," recently manifest in our decision to sell to it twelve FSE fighter planes.

A particular emphasis should, however, be placed on need in designing aid programs for this continent of the poorest. African nations constitute a vast laboratory for experimenting with ways of dealing with poverty—and a hopeful one in the sense that possibilities for development are not yet overrun by population. And in holding out as a group for aid to the poorest in the negotiations for a commodities agreement, the African nations have openly recognized the importance of this idea. Their own commitment to it might contribute to the broad political effect of U.S. aid extended on basic human needs criteria.

The influence garnered from multilateral economic cooperation is no easier to measure than that of bilateral aid. Institutional changes, as in removing trade barriers to processed raw materials, are often extended to the Third World as a whole rather than to Africa in particular. Even with World Bank or IDA loans to particular African countries, any connection with the achievement of our aims, say in southern Africa, is likely to be tenuous. But in the longer run, the degree of genuine U.S. effort to arrive at a meeting of minds with the nations of the Third World on New International Economic Order goals is likely to affect significantly the openness of Third World and African countries to the United States and to its values.

[239]

COMMUNICATING U.S. VALUES

In terms of U.S. policy, the communication of U.S. values (the third imperative) serves as means of confronting anti-Western ideologies, as well as an end in itself. Thus today the need for the United States to put forward its own view of a desirable future world and show the will to achieve it is at least as much a political as an idealistic goal.

Although this formulation may sound suspiciously like "making the world safe for democracy" or other evangelistic impulses that have gotten us into trouble in the past, I do not think there is much danger of excess in that direction now. We have come too far from the belief that our system is transferable—to a pervasive doubt that our political experience bears any point of contact with that of almost anyone else except our European allies. Now it seems that for the foreseeable future our form of democratic, capitalist system may not have much relevance to the needs of most Third World and African countries.

Our system's material fruits, however, its trade, various kinds of "expertise," and some technology, do have a good deal of relevance in the eyes of the developing world. And the importance of our continuing economic interaction with them will keep open the question of our values. Beyond this, the authority of the United States, and thus the magnetism of its model, depends on both the soundness of our domestic polity and the ability to focus on the points at which our values intersect with those of others.

The U.S. human rights campaign is an attempt to emphasize the importance to us of certain values which we feel are universally applicable. Our minimal standards (regarding arbitrary detention, torture and execution) do seem widely

[240]

applicable, and therefore consistent efforts to foster them should add to U.S. moral authority and thus to our influence. In Africa, as elsewhere in the world, this U.S. commitment is likely to be taken as evidence of a newly affirmative policy (replacing the elbows-up defensiveness toward the Third World that we have manifested for the past decade).

For Africa in particular, human rights means the end of white minority rule in southern Africa. Although it is evident to Africans that Carter's construction of "human rights" has more to do with Western standards regarding all governments' treatment of individual citizens than it does with their own problem, his emphasis on moral values has been impressive and inspiriting to the Africans in regard to their own cause. The two intersect in partially shared concepts about injustice. It is not too much to hazard that our efforts on behalf of the Africans' moral priority will turn their minds to the meaning and value of ours. In the same way, the U.S. drive for human rights in regard to Africa as to the rest of the Third World ought to be accompanied by a demonstrable commitment to the other main human rights priority of all the poor nations—that is, the achievement of certain basic *material* standards. Only then may our concern for their human rights seem to spring from genuine concern for their welfare rather than from efforts to counter their economic demands.

In this way, human rights become part of a whole vision of a world order. This vision will attract African adherents only insofar as it seems to answer their needs as well as ours, but as a manifestation of U.S. strength of purpose it will in itself increase U.S. authority and influence.

Not the least important aspect of this strategy is what must be frankly called public relations. Despite all good intentions and wise calculations about the U.S. national interest and about African realities, U.S. policy makers may find them-

[241]

selves forced into an effort to "counter the Soviets," in the Horn, for example, by media (and less-public) anxieties about "Soviet initiatives" in Ethiopia and "U.S. inaction." The administration must work full time to convey the realities underlying our policy: in the case of Ethiopia, to make clear that we are successfully keeping our options open while the Soviets (and Cubans) are becoming entrenched in various costly internal conflicts; that we can play an active diplomatic role while they cannot; that we are in full accord with African opinion on outside intervention, and that our relationships in Africa have improved thereby; that the possibility of productive U.S. relations with Ethiopia may not be far distant, and so on. In this way, rather than waiting to be forced into reaction, U.S. policy makers may educate press and public while preempting the critique from the cold warriors.

Having survived the spiritual upheavals of Vietnam, and surveying the world from a position of continuing economic superiority and some political advantage, we should have that sort of self-confidence. We should be able to maintain the dialectic, to balance in our minds short-term crises against long-term goals, the daily bouts in the U.S.-Soviet contest against long-range strategies. In Africa, our unavoidable concern about Soviet advances must not be allowed to push us into a short-sighted military competition played out on a field dimly viewed beyond our reactive activity. That contest we could lose; we cannot win it.

The reiteration here of the need to minimize the military competition in Africa and to pursue political and economic alternatives rooted in African realities springs, then, from a calculation of real U.S. options. This approach does not obviate day-to-day decision-making regarding the U.S.-Soviet competition and its military dimension. Nor, lamentably, does it diminish the importance of international public perceptions of

[242]

short-term U.S. and Soviet "wins" and "losses" for the stability of world order. In the short-term, however, it offers our best hope of minimizing the need for crisis-management. Over the long haul, it can help the United States advance the construction of a new and better international order.

NOTES

1. "U.S. Policy Toward Africa," speech of Secretary Cyrus Vance before the Annual Convention of the National Association for the Advancement of Colored People, July 1, 1977, St. Louis, Mo. Four months later, in a speech to the Johns Hopkins School of Advanced International Studies, Anthony A. K. Lake, Director of the Policy Planning Staff, again developed these themes in "Africa in a Global Perspective," October 27, 1977, Washington, D.C.

2. George Kennan's thoughts on "containment," enunciated in his "X" article in *Foreign Affairs*, July 1947, may have been codified into a theory not foreseen by its author. The term, as simplistically and commonly used, has come to be virtually synonymous with the military strategic obstruction of Soviet expansion wherever it might crop out. Thus construed, it has seemed to lead inevitably to a defensive reactiveness in which military means become paramount. It is in this sense that the term is used in this article. John Lewis Gaddis argues in "Containment: A Reassessment," *Foreign Affairs*, July 1977, pp. 873-87, that Kennan's own construction of the policy labeled by his coinage was both broader (in terms of means) and narrower (in terms of interest and geography). Although at the time he wrote the "X" article, Kennan almost undoubtedly would have placed Africa outside the sphere of interests upon which the United States should squander its resources, his emphasis on the importance of local nationalism, on pluralism, and the assertion of U.S. values has much to offer in a contemporary approach to Africa and the Third World.

3.   The statement of a State Department spokesman as paraphrased by Bernard Gwertzman in *The New York Times*. ("U.S. Steps Up Offers of Arms to Africans: Ready to Aid Sudan," July 28, 1977).

4.   "Resolution on Interference in the Internal Affairs of African States," Res. AHG85 (XIV), The Assembly of Heads of State and Government, Fourteenth Ordinary Session, Libreville, Gabon, July 2-5, 1977.

5.   Another order of military threat to the southern African region—and perhaps the most serious—is the reportedly imminent South African nuclear capability, which could be used to deter its black African neighbors or employed at a point of extreme desperation or nihilism. Alternatively, it could be brandished to undermine Western non-proliferation efforts.

6.   Both the character of the regime and parallel interests with those of various Western countries would be relevant in determining "importance."

7.   In the long run, the demonstrated effectiveness of aid in spurring development may be most important in justifying the expenditure to the U.S. Congress.

Index

Index

[245]